"Bart Baker's book is a must-read for anyone who wants to truly understand how to establish a breakthrough insurance agency. His model on how to multiply your income is not based on theory, but on years of hard work and personal experiences that will change the way you sell insurance. Baker is one of the top insurance agents at Farmers for a reason, and this book will help you understand how he built a thriving agency."

JEFF DAILEY
CEO, Farmers Insurance

"What an incredible book, which truly provides something valuable for every tenure of agency owner. From the individual just getting into the business, all the way to the agency owner with more than twenty years of experience, Baker's concepts and strategies will help agents achieve not only business success, but also what some might consider the unimaginable. Thank you for sharing!"

BILL MATLOCK
District Manager, Farmers Insurance

"Very insightful, Baker's book offers the blueprint for constructing a successful insurance agency that is built on exceeding the customer's expectations. A must-read."

WILLIAM WALRATH
Head of Southern California, Farmers Insurance

"Bart Baker is an out-of-the-box thinker who has used his creativity to build a great agency. He has developed a large group of loyal customers, all of whom have experienced the difference that an outstanding agent can provide."

FRANK SOLDANO
Territory Agency Manager, Southwest Territory, Farmers Insurance

"The Breakthrough Insurance Agency *is an in-depth guide to transforming an average insurance agency into a world-class agency with results that 'wow.' Baker's breakthrough system is designed to be a guiding light that will lead you on a proven path to success, regardless of where you are today or which market you are currently working in. By breaking down these essential elements, you will begin to understand, take action, become proficient, and master the ability to implement Baker's system in the different areas of your life and agency development.*

Baker leads the reader from mental readiness to the principles of preparing your agency for true transformation. He challenges the readers to expand their vision, improve their qualities, and understand the true benefits of agency growth. Baker demonstrates how he had to change and reinvent his agency in order to become one of the most powerful agencies in the Farmers Group, and how this can be done in any environment.

The book talks about enjoying the ride and choosing the people around you carefully. It challenges the readers to take a view of excellence in all that they do. It will be up to the reader to take advantage of the opportunity The Breakthrough Insurance Agency *has to offer and harness the power that Baker has given us in this wonderful book."*

THOMAS J. WHITE
President of Non-Insurance Business, Farmers Insurance

"A fantastic read for those entering the business or for those who want to take their business to the next level. 'Steal shamelessly' is my motto; seek out the best and do what they do. Bart Baker is one of the best."

MARTE FORMICO
Presidents Council District Manager, Farmers Insurance

"Bart Baker has written a must-read masterpiece in The Breakthrough Insurance Agency. *Not only does he give experienced insight on how to transform your business into a profitable enterprise, he also shares his experiences that will ultimately inspire you to take your business and life to the next level."*

STACY A. KORSGADEN
Presidents Council Agent, Farmers Insurance

"What a fantastic book! Bart Baker's The Breakthrough Insurance Agency is an honest account of many years of lessons learned and proven methods. It is a pathway that any agent can follow to mega success. Baker addresses both the mindset and structure to build an agency that stands the test of time, no matter the market. Reading this book is like sending nutrients straight to the roots of your agency. Baker's Gap Elimination Process™ and customer relationship ideology are both right on. In an industry that has been ransacked by those trying to turn insurance into a commodity, Baker gets right to the point and lays out a strategy to give you an unfair advantage over your competition. This book is a must-read for anyone in the insurance industry!"

GREG WINDHAM
Presidents Council District Manager, Farmers Insurance

"Entertaining and informative at the same time! Bart Baker gives clear, easy-to-follow, and practical guidance on how to build a breakthrough insurance agency. His advice is applicable for anyone wanting to grow exponentially and have fun at the same time. After reading the book, I found myself wondering why there weren't agencies like Baker's in every part of the county."

MARTIN MOLL
Partner, AKT LLP, CPAs and Business Consultants

"This book is a major breakthrough! Bart Baker makes the operation of an insurance agency more efficient and effective with the concepts in The Breakthrough Insurance Agency. Fundamentals are the key to success. The concepts described in this book are simple, without being simplistic. These pragmatic ideas and practices are a huge leap forward that will significantly improve your insurance agency's operation. I am completely motivated and empowered by this book. It is thought-provoking and enlightening, and it has refocused my thinking. I am confident that the information in this book will greatly improve my results in the future. An inspiring read."

GEORGE L. WEN
Presidents Council Agent, Farmers Insurance

"This powerful book is packed full of proven and practical tools and tips for any leader who wants to create sustainable, profitable growth over the long haul. The Breakthrough Insurance Agency is perfect for high performers, particularly those who are looking to break through and make their agency a profit center! Bart Baker offers real and practical insights for insurance agency owners. By utilizing his proven 3M Breakthrough System™ in conjunction with his Gap Elimination Process™, the performance of your business and your team will generate more business and revenue for you than ever before. Having known Baker quite a while, I can tell you his book will help you find that road to success you have been looking for! These strategies work, and this book has helped my team and me create winning processes for sustained profitable growth in our business."

JODY PREVATT
Presidents Council District Manager, Farmers Insurance

"Whether you're new or have spent twenty years in the insurance business, this book will help you not only think big but also achieve! From building out to executing your plan for success, it's all covered in The Breakthrough Insurance Agency."

MATT WOLK
Presidents Council District Manager, Farmers Insurance

"Bart Baker doesn't just take the concepts of people like Covey and Collins and turn them into practical real-life actions that an agent can use to build a successful business. He adds to this his own detailed success formula, which takes away all the excuses for potential failure and leaves the reader with a positive belief that 'what you think about comes about.' If you read Baker's book and follow his guiding principles and advice, everything you may have thought possible is possible!"

BRYAN MURPHY
President of Commercial Insurance, Farmers Insurance

The Breakthrough Insurance Agency

*How to Multiply Your Income,
Time and Fun*

Bart Baker, LUTCF

Think It Publishing
Malibu, California

The Breakthrough Insurance Agency
How to Multiply Your Income, Time and Fun

Bart Baker

Published by Think It Publishing, Malibu, California, USA
Copyright © 2015 by Bart Baker
All rights reserved.

Think It Publishing, LLC
29169 Heathercliff Road, Suite 208
Malibu, CA 90265-4183
(310) 457-5092
Bart@bwbaker.com

Limit of Liability/Disclaimer of Warranty:

Publishing manager: Helen Chang, www.authorbridgemedia.com
Editor: Kristine Serio, www.authorbridgemedia.com
Publishing assistant: Carla Baker
Cover and Interior design: Peri Poloni-Gabriel, www.knockoutbooks.com

Library of Congress Control Number: 2015905470

ISBN: 978-0-9960552-4-6
ISBN (hardcover): 978-0-9960552-3-9
ISBN: (e-book): 978-0-9960552-5-3

Ordering information:
Quantity sales. Special discounts are available on quantity purchases by corporations, associations, and others. For details, contact the publisher at the address above.

Printed in the United States of America

Dedication

To the joy of my life and the best friend
a man could want: my wife, Wendy.

Also to my children, Jaime, Amber, and Brian;
my four amazing grandsons, Jake, Jonah, Julian, and Luca; my
mother, Elaine, and second mother, Norma;
my brother, Ben; my sister, Celeste; my late brother, Beau;
and finally, my father.

I love each of you, and I thank you for all of your love and
support. I am a better man because of you.

◦⟭⟭⟬⟬◦

Table of Contents

Acknowledgments

As with most things in my life, I have to start with thanking my wife, Wendy. To be married to the love of my life, who also happens to be my business partner, is a real blessing.

A huge thank you goes out to my book team, headed by Helen Chang of Author Bridge Media, project assistant Carla Baker, designer Peri Poloni-Gabriel with Knockout Design, illustrator John-Luke Fredericks with The Drawshop, and my assistant Vanessa Angers. You've all done an amazing job!

I believe that every good insurance agent has had an equally good district manager in his or her life. I'm grateful that my original district manager found me through that tiny ad in the *Fire Department* magazine and showed me the opportunity so persuasively that it caused me to take action. Don McNew was the catalyst for a huge change in my life.

Thank you to the leaders of Farmers, starting with Martin Feinstein, Paul Hopkins, Bob Woudstra, and Jeff Dailey, who have been amazing stewards of this great company. The fact that they make themselves personally available, even while running this huge company, makes this feel like a family business. After twenty-seven years, I am grateful to be part of the Farmers family.

A man is only as good as his team, and I have the best there is. The people at B.W. Baker Insurance are second to none. My gratitude goes to my business partner and wife, Wendy; our commercial lines department with Florence, Bianca, and Sara; our personal lines department with Maria, Kristen, Jorge, and Virginia; our life and health department with Vanessa, Dulce, and Nessa; and our front office and claims department with Kim. I am so fortunate to have you all in my life.

Last, but not least, are the clients that I've had the privilege to serve. I cannot think of many businesses in which the transition from client to friend can occur so seamlessly. I can honestly say I don't go to work; I go to a great office and hang out with people I truly love, and I talk with friends all day long.

∽

Introduction

Opportunity Knocks

They say that when opportunity knocks, you should answer the door. But that's not always as easy as it sounds.

Right now, you may be looking at the wonderful opportunity of building an insurance agency. Maybe you've met a number of people who are really successful in this business, and you want to be one of them. You see how insurance can be a vehicle for everything you want for you and your family, both personally and professionally.

At the same time, maybe you're feeling overwhelmed by the task ahead of you. Maybe you earned your license, and when they handed it to you they said, "Congratulations. You now have a license to sell insurance."

And you said to yourself, *Okay . . . so where do I start?*

Or maybe you've been in the business for five or ten years. You've figured out a lot of stuff, and you're already doing pretty well. But maybe you still see room for improvement in your agency. Maybe you're trying to figure out how to retain good people and build a strong team that's in it for the long haul. Maybe you just can't seem to remove yourself from the day-to-day operations of the business, even though you've been trying to for years. You want to transition from a market-driven agency to one that is referral-based instead, but you don't know how.

Maybe you've even been selling insurance for upward of ten to fifteen years. You're making money, and you're doing fine by most people's standards. You have systems in place that give you dependable results. You're bringing in a great income, and there's nothing wrong with that. But maybe you've plateaued, and the business just isn't as exciting as it used to be.

Wherever you happen to be on the journey, the situation is the same: you're looking for a future that's bigger and brighter than your past.

You may not have all the answers yet, but you're excited about the opportunity in your hands. Because you know that, provided you can figure it out, this business has the ability to get you to where you want to go. You know that you don't need to find a different vehicle to take you there. You've seen it in the successful agents around you. Insurance has what it takes to help you accomplish your hopes and dreams.

If this sounds like you, then I have some good news. You're in the right place.

The Breakthrough

Whether you're a new or experienced agent, you're in the right business. The insurance business is amazing. I can tell you from experience that you will definitely achieve the success you're looking for using insurance as your vehicle, as long as you're willing to roll up your sleeves and get things going. There's just no question about it.

Your insurance agency has the potential to give you the breakthrough you've been searching for.

I've been where you've been. I know what it's like. In fact, I remember it like it was yesterday. When I was starting out, I had the opportunity to talk to some great agents who had already found success. One of them, Steve Barrett, invited me to visit his office in California's San Fernando Valley. To me, that business looked like the office of the future. It was a big place. Steve had ten people on staff, and they handled thousands of policies.

Seeing that office was motivating for me, but it was also intimidating. *Okay, that's where I want to be,* I thought. *But it seems so far away. I don't even remotely know how to get from where I am to where this guy is.*

All I knew was that I needed to figure it out. It was just my wife, Wendy, and me in our business. We put our heads together and started thinking. One baby step led to the next. Gradually, we learned what needed to happen to get the ball rolling. And we worked the rest out from there, piece by piece and year after year.

Now, I'm not perfect. When I started out, I didn't get everything right on the first try. I struggled like crazy. But in the end, after decades of trial, error, and persistence, Wendy and I figured out the things that worked for us. And I really believe that they will work for you, too.

My Road to Insurance

Wendy and I are the founders of B.W. Baker Insurance Services in Malibu, California. Today, our business is one of the most successful breakthrough insurance agencies in the country. But it took decades of hard work and learning the ropes to achieve that dream.

Wendy and I moved to Malibu in 1979 because we wanted to raise our kids in a good community. When we first arrived, we rented a garage in someone's house and fixed it up as our home.

Both of us worked hard. I had a job in the Los Angeles County Fire Department, sometimes spending four or five days at a time away from home. Meanwhile, Wendy worked two jobs as a bank teller and running a maid agency.

Eventually, we were able to move out of the garage and into a low-income housing townhome. By then, our third child was on the way, and there wasn't enough room for all of us in the condo. It seemed that no matter how hard we worked, we were trapped in a hand-to-mouth existence.

Life was not fun. It was just work. I didn't want to live that way, and I knew it wasn't the kind of life I wanted for my wife and kids.

That was when I found insurance.

The idea appeared as an ad in one of the magazines at the fire department. It sounded like it had a lot of potential. I showed the opportunity to Wendy, and she agreed that it was the right thing to do.

I got my license, and we rented out a little 300-square-foot office. At first we didn't know what we were doing. We had to figure things out. But slowly and surely, it began to work. We started bringing in an extra $500 a month. Gradually, that number grew.

Our real breakthrough came about eighteen months into the business, when I got a call from someone asking if I could insure a Rolls Royce.

I was to meet the person at the Beverly Hills Hotel in Beverly Hills. When I got there and asked for Bill, the attendant took me down to the basement.

Bill was seated in a little office the size of a broom closet. When I arrived, he handed me a file. "Everything you need to come up with a quote should be in here," he explained. "My insurance is expiring at the end of the week, and I'd really like to get your quote pretty quickly."

"Sure," I said, "absolutely."

When I got back to my office and opened the file, I found that Bill didn't have just one Rolls Royce to cover. He was the personal representative for a sultan, and that folder contained a whole fleet of Rolls Royces that needed insurance—fast. It was the biggest thing I'd ever seen.

I stayed up late into the night, quoting one Rolls Royce after another, double- and triple-checking the package as I put it together. The grand total came out to $150,000. And the next day, when I brought the quote back to Bill, he didn't even hesitate. He pulled out a checkbook and wrote me a check for the full $150,000 right on the spot.

As I left the Beverly Hills Hotel that day, my head was spinning. I couldn't believe that I just sold a policy for $150,000. For the first time, I understood that there were people out there who paid a lot of money for their insurance. I realized that I needed to figure out how to be the type of agent who would attract that type of client. I needed to serve that end of the market.

So Wendy and I set out to accomplish that mission. And the resulting journey took us further than we'd ever imagined we could go.

Tried and True

Every industry has its accolades and awards. The carrier that our agency writes with is Farmers Insurance, and we've been honored to achieve every recognition Farmers has to offer. Toppers is an award given to agencies in the top 15 percent of production, and we've gotten that every single year since we opened. We've earned Championship—the top 3 percent of producers—for eighteen of the twenty-five years we've been open.

After I retired from the fire department to focus on the insurance agency full time, we achieved Presidents Council. It is the highest award Farmers offers; it recognizes those who are in the top 1 percent. We've gotten the Presidents Council award every year since 2002. We've also made Court of the Table and Top of the Table several times—two of the most prestigious accolades in the financial services industry at the million-dollar round table.

Our business is consistently in the top 1 percent of Farmers agencies in the nation as far as income, bringing in $20 million a year in gross written premium in 2014. As of 2015, we had more than eight thousand policies in force, and about 80 percent of our policies service the higher end of the market place.

Our agency is comprehensive and runs like clockwork. As of 2015, we employ fourteen people, and we have departments for life insurance, health insurance, contact managers, personal lines, commercial lines, claims concierge, and the front office. We have one of the most consistent and profitable track records in the nation.

I share this with you only as a point of reference. Wendy and I didn't achieve all this because we were luckier or more brilliant than other people in the industry. We started at square one, and we faced every challenge you can imagine along the way, from figuring out the basics to fine-tuning the system as it grew.

If you are going through some of the challenges we've experienced, I want you to know that you can overcome them to achieve amazing things. I've walked in your shoes, and I know what you're going through. Even though we had some great mentors, Wendy and I had to work things out the hard way. I can't tell you how many times I wished that we'd had some written guidelines to help us along the road.

That's why I wrote this book.

Your Breakthrough Blueprint

I've been blessed with success in my business and in my life. *The Breakthrough Insurance Agency* is my way of giving back. I know what it's like to be a new agent. I know the kinds of struggles that more advanced agents face with their agencies. Now, I want to share with you some of the tools, systems, and concepts that I've learned from my almost three decades in this business.

My road to breakthrough had its share of sweat and tears. You're going to have to work for yours, too. But I believe that you can shave years and years off of your journey to getting you and your family to where you aspire to be, just by not trying to reinvent the wheel all on your own. That's where I can help.

There are many paths to success in the insurance business. The system in this book is the one that worked for me. As long as you're looking to improve on your situation—whether you're new and struggling or you're already doing great and want to do even better—

I really believe that the concepts and tools in these chapters will help you reach your goals.

It doesn't matter what stage of the game you're at. As long as you are truly motivated to create a bigger and better future for yourself, the systems in this book will work. You can do this.

The Breakthrough Insurance Agency can help.

*The starting point
of all achievement
is desire.*

—**NAPOLEON HILL**

Chapter 1

Your Breakthrough Insurance Agency

Your Breakthrough Insurance Agency

What is a breakthrough insurance agency?

A breakthrough insurance agency is one that performs significantly better than the peer group it's measured against. I'm not talking about your run-of-the-mill type of success here. When you have a breakthrough insurance agency on your hands, people will actually look at it and say, "Wow, look at them. They've really broken through."

With the system in this book, you will transform your business into a breakthrough insurance agency. And when you do, you'll reap the rewards. Because a breakthrough insurance agency multiplies your income, time, and fun.

When I say this model multiplies your income, I mean it. I'm not talking about making 10 or 20 percent more than what you're currently bringing in. I'm talking about doubling, tripling, or quadrupling your income—and beyond.

You won't have to put in loads of late nights to make that income rise happen, either, because this system also multiplies your time by using the services of others. In fact, with this system, you're going to work less. You're going to get a much higher return on the energy you put into your business by becoming more efficient.

And once that happens, you're really going to start having some fun. You'll spend your days coming up with new ideas to help your business prosper even more, and you'll have the free time you need to have the lifestyle you want. Because enjoyment is always the goal in the end. I'm not interested in working eighty-hour weeks and taking my money to my grave, and I bet you're not either. You want to enjoy a life of abundance right now. And I can promise you, whatever dreams you have in mind, your breakthrough insurance agency will be able to fund them.

Using the strategies in this book, your opportunities for success are truly unlimited.

So, who can build a breakthrough insurance agency? What kind of market will support it? And what are the fundamental rules you need to know before you roll up your sleeves and dive in?

The Breakthrough Insurance Agent

It doesn't matter who you are or where you stand right now. As long as your goal is to build a multiline agency that can service all of your clients' needs, and as long as you have a desire to improve, the systems and strategies I teach in these chapters will work for you.

I've coached scores of agents from all kinds of backgrounds, and I've seen them achieve incredible success using these techniques. I myself used them to build a life of abundance from almost nothing. I know agents in this business who make $10,000 a month. I know agents who make $50,000, $100,000, and $150,000 a month on a regular basis, year in and year out. No two of them are exactly the same. But they used a form of this system to get where they are today.

The strategies in this book will work for any agent, anywhere, at any stage of the game. If you're just getting into the business, sticking to this protocol will get you off to a quicker start and help you obtain greater success in the shortest possible amount of time. If you're an existing agent—especially one who has plateaued—putting these systems in place will rocket you to the next level of achievement.

And all of this is true for you in any market.

The Breakthrough Market

The breakthrough market is simple: it is the higher end of what's available in your area.

No matter where you live, your client base runs the gamut from the lower to the upper end. You want to target the higher end of your market. This doesn't mean that there's anything wrong with the people on the lower end. It's just much more effective to attract and market to the higher end of your client base, because not only do these people have more to insure, but they're also going to be more interested in two of the key things you'll be offering: incredible service and being insured correctly, rather than cheaply.

When you focus your energy on a breakthrough market, you will set yourself up for continuous growth—even in a bad economy. I can say this from experience. During the recession in the late 2000s, when many people were hunkering down and cutting costs, I was able to invest in my business and double our income.

With the breakthrough system, your agency won't be affected by the whims of the financial market. It will be supported by the strategies you've built it with—and the philosophy behind the service that you provide.

The Breakthrough Philosophy

The core philosophy of the breakthrough system is this: when you build and maintain solid relationships with your client base, your agency will thrive.

If this isn't the way that you're currently doing business, you're in for a big mental shift. You're going to have to stop funneling hours of time and energy into marketing and cold calling people out of the phone book. I tried that "quote and hope" strategy myself during my first year in business, and those were the days when I had pennies in my pocket.

Instead, you're going to focus on building relationships and creating strong centers of influence. There is a way of doing business that is 100 percent relationship driven, and it will lead to one critical benefit that will change the way you sell insurance forever: referrals.

We all know that it's much easier to do and maintain business with people who are referred to us by friends, family members, and associates. Using my breakthrough system, you can actually take your agency to the point where the phone rings all day long with people who are interested in talking to you about insurance.

I'll go into detail on developing referrals later in this book, but the underlying fact remains: without strong relationships, you don't get referrals. Base your business on putting people first. When you do, and when you support it using the systems I'm about to teach you, you will thrive.

The Breakthrough System

The concepts in these chapters aren't just designed to help you survive in the insurance business. They're designed to make you thrive. When you take them to heart, they will shave years and years off of your path to success.

To achieve your personal breakthrough in the insurance industry, you will need:

✓ *Vision.* Like any venture in life, the path to a breakthrough insurance agency begins with a powerful vision. In this chapter, you'll learn how to create a vision that fuels your motivation and helps you overcome any obstacles you encounter along the way to success.

✓ *Qualities.* To thrive in the insurance business, you need to hone three key qualities: likability, confidence, and trustworthiness. I'll give you the guidelines you need to assess and develop these qualities in yourself on an ongoing basis.

✓ *Growth.* You need to grow to become a breakthrough insurance agency, but growth isn't something you pull out of a hat. You have to fund it—and you have to fund it right. This chapter will outline a surefire plan that will fund continuous growth in your agency, and show you how you can reward yourself along the way.

✓ *The 3M Breakthrough System™: Maximizers, Multipliers, and Measurement.* Maximizers and multipliers are the people you'll be bringing onto your team as your agency continues to expand. In this chapter, you'll learn how to leverage both of these positions and define success with measurement, in order to detangle yourself from your agency's day-to-day operations and maximize your benefits.

✓ *The Gap Elimination Process*™. You're going to need a major edge to put your agency a cut above the competition. That edge is the Gap Elimination Process™ (GEP). I'll walk you through my GEP system and tell you how you can guarantee faultless coverage for your clients, every time.

✓ *Departments.* As your breakthrough agency grows, you'll be able to make it even more efficient by structuring your business with departments. I'll take you through the nuts and bolts of how to do this right.

✓ *Fine-Tuning.* With the basic structure of your business in place, you're ready to take it to the next level with some fine tuning. This chapter will give you a wealth of tips and tricks to build your credibility and put your agency two more steps ahead of the competition.

✓ *Referrals.* Referrals are the lifeblood of your breakthrough insurance agency. I'll teach you how to attract them in the first place and keep them coming in by rewarding the individuals who funnel business your way.

✓ *Compensation.* Your agency is only as strong as your team, and that means you need to compensate these people fairly. In this chapter, I'll give you a complete compensation structure for your staff that lets them share in the success of the business and encourages team members to stick with you for the long term.

✓ *Vision Now.* With the protocol under your belt, I'll show you exactly where to start building your breakthrough insurance agency, whether you're a new agent or an experienced one.

These concepts have been structured and refined by not only me personally, but also the scores of agents I've coached over the years. We've put each and every one of them to the test from every angle imaginable—and we've always come out on top in the end.

You're next.

Shake off the Shackles

This book is a road map. It will take you to the success you want in a very short period of time. When you act on the concepts in these chapters, you will see dramatic results—not only in your income, but also in the lifestyle that you achieve for yourself and your family.

If you find yourself shackled and enslaved to your business, you'll learn how to make your business work for you instead. By the time you're done here, you will have more money on your hands and less stress in your brain. You will have the freedom to do what you want, when you want to do it. You will have fun going to work every day.

You will have a breakthrough insurance agency—one that will expand with your vision to give you the life of your dreams.

But your vision can't expand until you have a great vision to begin with. In the next chapter, I'll take you through this first critical step of the breakthrough system and show you how to leverage it for enormous gain in your business and life.

⌒⟪⟫⌒

Chapter 2

Visualize Your Breakthrough

Full Circle

In 2014, I had a birthday celebration at our house.

The party was beautifully catered by a five-star caterer, with the bartenders and servers dressed in nice, black uniforms. Our house is located above the beach, and we had a long, ornately decorated table for twenty-six set up overlooking the ocean. Seated at that table were the president and CFO of Farmers, the president of Commercial, the district managers and agents I'd gotten to know, and all of my family and friends.

We had the most amazing meal together. We told great stories, and we drank great wine. It was a celebration I could have only dreamed about years earlier. I remembered our start in the community, renting a garage just so we could raise our kids in a good neighborhood, and struggling to make ends meet.

Even back then, when we lived in that garage and it felt like the monthly payments to the orthodontist for our kids' braces would never end, I had a vision of prosperity. I saw achievement in my life, and when I started my insurance agency, I brought that vision to my business. Now, with this birthday celebration, I felt that I had come full circle.

That party was a real manifestation of my vision of my own success.

Vision: The Core of Success

If you're not looking for something, you're not going to find it.

Vision is the act of looking. It's the "ask" part of the saying "ask and you shall receive." A lot of people think vision and goals are the same thing, but that's not true. A goal is something concrete and measurable—like earning a million dollars. A vision is a direction—like having a thriving, prosperous agency. You need both goals and vision to achieve success. But it's the vision that makes the success fun, worthwhile, and sweet.

When you have vision, you set the intention to do or achieve something, solely because you would like to do or achieve it. You don't have to have any other validation. A vision is something that belongs only to you—and that's good enough.

Nothing happens without vision. If you just go to work and start implementing processes and procedures without having a vision of where you want to go, you might do some business, but you won't have the enjoyment that should come along with it. You won't reach your full potential. Because you can get in the ring every day and fight the good fight, but if you're not fighting with an end game in mind, you're going to get the life beat out of you with nothing to show for it. There's no joy in that type of life.

But if you have vision, you open your imagination to the lifestyle you want to have in the future. Once you come up with your vision, work becomes energizing and fun, because you know that the effort you're putting forth is going to help you achieve what you're looking for. Everything is so much more gratifying and interesting because you know there's an end game.

And not only is vision a lot of fun, but the more ingrained your vision is in your mind, the easier it becomes to find the opportunities to support it. In this chapter, I'll show you how to create a strong and multifaceted vision—and how to use it to help you overcome lulls in your business.

"What You Think about Comes About"

My favorite expression is "what you think about comes about."

It sounds simple, but it's really profound. It means that whatever thoughts you maintain predominantly in your mind are the things that will materialize. If your head is full of doom and gloom, you're going to manifest a doom-and-gloom lifestyle. But if you continually focus on thoughts of prosperity, your life will manifest good things.

That's powerful. It's an aspect of vision that you have total control over at all times. You cannot think negatively and expect a positive outlook. And it sounds easy, but I'll be the first to admit that in practice it's harder to do than you might think—especially on those days when everything is going wrong.

So what can you do to keep yourself thinking positively?

Pay attention to the details. What are you reading and looking at? What are your health habits? Who are you hanging out with? Every little thing fits into the bigger picture of your vision, and one choice affects all the others. Make the tough decisions to remove the bad things and people from your sphere of influence and replace them with good alternatives. The more you stay on top of the little things you feed your mind, the more attuned you'll be to massive success.

I personally find it beneficial to have positive thought processes prepared and ready to go for those moments when I find myself getting into a negative space. I'll be out on a walk and I'll repeat a mantra: "I am healthy, I am happy, I am prosperous." It doesn't sound life-changing, but you know, after repeating that for seven or eight minutes, it actually changes my state of mind. And I'm back to the races.

Figure out some positive thought processes that work for you. Then use them to keep your vision in the forefront of your mind, so that "what you think about comes about."

Expand Your Vision

A vision isn't static. Whatever vision you set forth today, it's important to realize that that vision is not set in stone. You can and should expand upon it as you continue to achieve milestones.

An expanding vision keeps you excited about what you do every day. It keeps you moving forward. As long as you have something new to look forward to and achieve, you're a lot less likely to hit a lull in your business. You'll just keep continuing on that upward trajectory.

I used this concept of expanding vision as I worked toward the different industry awards offered by Farmers. When I started out, I wanted to make Toppers Club—a big achievement that was nonetheless at the lower end of the awards list. Once I made Toppers, I didn't stop and sit on my laurels. I said, "Okay, we did that. What's next?" The next award on the ladder was Championship, so that became my new vision. And after we earned championship, I expanded the vision again to Presidents Council.

It took us quite some time to achieve Presidents Council. That was a really big step. But because I had that vision, everything we did was designed to achieve it. And sure enough, we earned it in the end. I don't think we would have achieved Presidents Council if I hadn't intentionally set that vision to try to achieve it.

Set your vision high to begin with. Then let it take you even higher.

Well-Rounded Vision

As your vision expands, keep in mind that you want it to be well rounded.

By all means, have a vision for your business—and every area of your business as it relates to gross income, staff, the type of clientele that you want, the number of policies you have, the location of your office, and what you want your work day to look like. But keep in mind that there's more to life than the business. You want your vision to include your personal life as well—your health, family and friends, community, spiritual well-being, and anything else that's important to you.

When I first started my agency, I would leave for work at seven o'clock in the morning and get home at ten o'clock at night. I'd work weekends; I just did whatever it took, no matter what.

I don't do that anymore. Because now my vision is to be home at six o'clock to have dinner with my wife. A lot of people in my position work constantly, and that's fine if that's what you *want* to do. But you don't *have* to do it that way. You can support the type of lifestyle you want with a work schedule that feels enjoyable to you.

There's really no limitation when it comes to vision, and you don't have to confine yourself to one vision alone. Dream in multivision. As long as it's something you personally want to achieve, and as long as it's not hurting anybody else, the more things you bring into your well-rounded vision, the happier and more energized you'll be.

Don't believe the saying that "You can't have your cake and eat it too." You really can have it all. And since that's the case, let me tell you—I would eat that cake.

Vision: Not Always What It Seems

Just because you have a vision doesn't mean that it's always going to manifest exactly the way you imagined it. Sometimes, vision has its own ideas about how it wants to expand.

I do believe your vision will always be fulfilled eventually, given time. But it may not always look just like you described it. What will always come about is the underlying desire beneath the vision.

For example, maybe you have a vision of prosperity, abundance, and security. In your head, those things look a certain way. Maybe you're thinking of a specific amount of money in the bank, or a fleet of yachts anchored in the bay, or a castle in a specific location. Well, if you fast-forward into the future, you might not be living in that castle or hanging out in those yachts, but you'll realize that the same amount of prosperity, abundance, and security have found you anyway—just in a different form.

At the end of the day, the physical manifestation isn't really that important. It's the heart of the vision that counts.

Share the Vision

A great way to help your vision come to pass is to share it with others—with both those who are higher up on the achievement ladder than you and also your team. I really believe the saying that "birds of a feather flock together." It's incredibly important to make sure that the people you associate with are like-minded and supportive of you, because you really are the mean average of the five people whom you spend the most time with.

Sharing my vision was a big part of the reason that I achieved Presidents Council with Farmers. I made it very well known to anybody I thought could be helpful that this was what I was striving to achieve. Now, the executives I talked to understood that if you get to Presidents Council, you're doing a lot of business, and that definitely benefits the company. So of course they were happy to share with me the knowledge and resources they had.

When I shared my vision of making Presidents Council with my staff, it was about the journey. I explained what it meant for the agency to earn that award, and why it was important to all of us. It wasn't so much that we'd achieve the end goal. It was what achieving that goal would make of *us* in the process. The entire team had to rise to the occasion of becoming Presidents Council material. We learned what type of production a Presidents Council agency has, how they are typically staffed, and the benefits of membership in that club.

The entire team focused on it. Everyone knew the goal and was working toward it. Everything we did was prefaced by, "What would a Presidents Council agency do in this situation?"

It was one of the proudest moments in my career when we were told we'd made it. That achievement was the collective accomplishment of the entire team. Our vision had materialized.

When you articulate your vision to people who are in a position to support you, you will put a foundation under that vision much more quickly than you'd be able to otherwise.

Persistent Vision

When you find yourself and your business in a lull, you can use your vision to pull you out of the rut and start making progress again.

If you're experiencing a lull, it means that your vision isn't clear enough to provide you with a direction to move forward. Maybe you've even achieved your original vision, but you haven't yet expanded it to something bigger and brighter. You're going to work and going through the motions, but you're not able to state whether the goals you set to reach your vision are on track.

When you find yourself in that position, take note of your state of mind. What are your predominant thoughts? Are you thinking thoughts that are serving you, or are you in a negative state, coming from a mental place of lack and scarcity? If you're in a negative state, turn yourself around. Get yourself thinking positive thoughts about how capable you are, how your agency is growing, and how much your clients love you.

Then take a look at your goals. I mentioned earlier that you need goals to support your vision, and that's absolutely true. Do your concrete, measurable goals support your vision? If so, are they on track? Check in with those and see how you're actually doing. Then make a plan to move forward.

Remember that as long as you're still alive, you haven't failed.

You're still working toward your vision. You're still moving forward. Even if you're not growing as quickly as you'd like, keep that in mind. You're not done.

Envision Success

If you are really looking to find significant success, I'm not going to sugarcoat it: it takes a lot of effort and hard work. Vision is the tool that keeps you on course in the middle of all that—and gives you the opportunity to have a lot of fun along the way.

In the end, we're all looking for happiness. Happiness is the gradual achievement of your vision. As you reach benchmarks, achieve your original vision, and then create new visions to build on the old ones, you will bring a tremendous amount of satisfaction to your life.

I can tell you beyond a shadow of a doubt that if you set a vision and continue to "ask" for it, then you will receive. When you get right down to it, this is one of the most fundamental universal laws. So many people have things they want to do, and they think, "This would be nice." But they never take it to the point where they actually ask. They never set a vision for themselves. And they miss out on their dreams because of it.

Never make that mistake. Set your vision high, keep it growing, and never give up on it. That's the cornerstone of success with your agency. But as powerful as it is, vision isn't the only tool you have at your disposal. In the next chapter, I'll take you through the key qualities you need to take your business to incredible heights.

౭ೲಲ

Chapter 3

The Three Personal Breakthrough Qualities™

An Expensive Education

Your core qualities aren't just something you talk about. They're values that you actually believe in and adhere to, even when that's a hard decision to make.

One day in 2010, a high-end client of ours called the office. He'd purchased insurance from us the year before to cover a house that he was custom building. Now he needed a new policy.

"I'm going to be putting the home up for sale," he told us, "and I want to stage it. So I need to insure about $100,000 worth of furniture."

We figured it out for him, and I had my commercial manager work out the details. The manager was a great team member whom I trusted and had a confident relationship with; she'd been with us for about ten years. "Just make sure theft is included in the policy," I told her.

She took care of it and came back to me with the report. "I spoke to underwriting," she said. "They told me that theft is included, and everything is fine. We're good to go."

Somewhere in the back of my mind, I felt a little uncomfortable that we didn't have that confirmation in writing yet. But I dismissed it. "Okay, great," I said. "Just note who you talked to in the file." And she did.

Six weeks later, the client called us up again. "Bart," he said, "I'm sure glad we got that insurance, because somebody broke into the house over the weekend. They stole $23,000 worth of stuff we rented to stage the home."

"All right," I told him, "no problem." And we filed the claim.

That claim came back denied.

The client got the denial notice in the mail and called me up again. "So Bart . . ." he said, "What's going on with this letter I just received? They're telling me I'm not covered for theft."

It turned out that there had been a misunderstanding when we set up the policy in the first place. We called the rep that my commercial manager had spoken to, but nothing could be done other than filing an error and omission claim, and I knew that that would be a long, laborious, and frustrating process for my client. I wasn't going to put him through that. At the end of the day, it was my problem, not his.

I called him back.

"Look," I said, "I'm terribly sorry about this. There's been a misunderstanding, and the insurance won't cover your claim. But listen, I told you that you have coverage; therefore, you have coverage." If the policy had been valid, the insurer would have covered $18,000 after the client's $5,000 deductible. So I wrote out a check for $18,000 from my personal account, and within twenty-four hours I had delivered it to him personally.

That financial hit hurt at the time, but it was the right thing to do. The client was a businessman, and he appreciated my way of operating. He began doing more business with me than ever, and within eighteen months I had made up the money I lost. He's also sent me numerous referrals, and there is no question that I've made many, many times over the amount of money that I put down for his claim that day.

The Three Personal Breakthrough Qualities™

Having strong core qualities and being absolutely committed to them will do more for your business than you can possibly imagine.

Everyone needs a set of strong guiding principles. I've found that three personal core qualities in particular are key to building a breakthrough insurance agency: likability, confidence, and trustworthiness.

These three personal qualities are absolutely foundational. They are the building blocks that will give you tremendous success in this business. You can implement all of the systems that I'm going to show you in the rest of this book and be dynamite with every one of them, but if you don't have these three traits mastered down to a science, nothing else will work out.

Why is that?

When people like you, feel confident in your knowledge, and trust you, you will get their business almost every time. On the other hand, if they don't feel that you're likable, confident, and trustworthy, you're not going to get very far. It's that simple.

You might think there are a lot of other important personal qualities you need to be successful, and you would be right. But these three breakthrough qualities are the ones you need to focus on as the center of influence in your business, because you are the pivotal person within your agency. You can delegate things like organization and technical excellence, because you're not going to be doing things like quoting, issuing, binding, servicing, and so on.

But you can't delegate that first personal touch you have with new clients. You can't delegate the likability, confidence, and trustworthiness that happens during that initial transference of emotion. You're responsible for that first impression, and even though it takes less time than everything that happens on the back end, it carries more weight. The client needs to know that there's a competent figurehead who is in charge of the whole system.

Your end game is not to run the detailed processes of your business. Your end game is to manage a customer relationship with these personal core qualities as your guide. Period.

With that in mind, let's take a closer look at the qualities themselves: likability, confidence, and trustworthiness.

The Likability Factor

With insurance, the client isn't just buying a policy. He or she is buying you as an agent. And the first hurdle you have to pass before that transaction can happen is the likability test.

All things being equal, the client has to like you. If the client doesn't like you, he or she is certainly not going to buy from you. But if the client likes you, your job becomes immensely easier. You can put yourself in a position where even if your product isn't as competitive as someone else's, the client buys from you anyway because he or she likes you more than the other agent.

So likability is at the very top of the breakthrough qualities list.

Without being likable, you'll never get the chance to demonstrate your confidence in your policies or your trustworthiness. The more likable you are, the more orders you're probably going to bring in. And the great thing is that even if you already consider yourself a likable person, you can keep building on your likability factor. So where do you start building likability with a new client?

You start by finding the commonality that will help you bond with that person.

This is one reason I really prefer to meet a new client in person. If it's a personal lines type of transaction like home or umbrella insurance, I'll meet them at their house, and typically they'll show me around. While we're walking, I'll see pictures of the wife and kids. I have kids myself, so I'll strike up a conversation. Right away, we have some common ground, and that creates the likability factor.

The commonality doesn't have to be family-based. If you're into sports cars, and the person has a sports car, you can talk about cars. If you like wine, and the customer has a wine cellar, there's your common ground. You find it, and whatever it is, for a while you are definitely not talking about insurance. You are talking about real human things—things that inspire the client to think, "I like this person. Not only can I do business with him, but I could even be his friend."

If you can't meet the client in person, you can still find a commonality from talking to him or her over the phone. One of my favorite ways to do this is to say, "Hey, it's Thursday. The weekend's coming up, what do you have planned?" And most people will tell you. From that, you can find a way to continue the conversation.

You'll be able to feel the moment when the likability bond kicks in. If you haven't felt it, then it hasn't happened yet. Just be patient and wait for it. Don't make the mistake of knocking on the door and getting straight to business. The personal connection comes first.

Be genuine, and stay conscious of the likability factor. Ask yourself, "Does this person like me? How can I improve upon that likability relationship?" Once you have likability on your side, it will take you a long way.

Confidence That Counts

Once you have likability under your belt, confidence is the next key personal quality you need in order to grow your relationship with a client.

You need to have confidence in yourself, your products, and your business. People want to do business with an agent who is confident and knows what he or she is talking about. You're talking about protecting their assets, everything they own—their homes, cars, liability exposure, and life insurance. They're not going to entrust all of that to someone who looks uncertain or incapable.

Confidence is something that people pick up on just by being around you. You can tell if someone is confident or not by the way they speak and carry themselves. In other words, your potential clients are picking up on your confidence level before you even say "hello." And you need to make sure that they intuitively pick up on the fact that you know what you're talking about right away, even before you start talking about package details.

Keep in mind that at this stage, everything matters when it comes to confidence. First impressions are crucial. How you dress, the cleanliness of your car, and how you shake hands all make a difference. Do you have a firm handshake and look the client in the eye? Are you able to have a good conversation? These are the kinds of things that will help the client intuitively pick up on your confidence.

Another key way to build your confidence as an agent is to know every one of your policies 100 percent, backward and forward. That means you've read and understood the language as a legal contract. If there was something you didn't understand, you took action to find out what it meant. That way, when you're talking to someone about a policy, you never have to worry that there will be a question you can't answer.

Remember that you're not coming from a place of trying to make a sale. You're coming from a position of being an expert in the business. You've read your policies, you know your policies—you may even own some of the policies yourself. You've seen how the policies have impacted people who were insured both properly and not properly, and you can say, "This is what you need based upon my experience and expertise in the business."

When you transfer this kind of confidence to your clients, they will be much more likely to buy what you recommend. And that's good for both them and your business.

True-Blue Trust

So now you're very likeable. Now you have a high level of confidence, because you put in the hard work of understanding all the details of your policies. At this point, you're ready to bring the last of the three core qualities into play: trustworthiness.

Trustworthiness is a critical follow-up to confidence, because confidence can be misleading. People can do absolutely horrible things when they use their confidence to persuade others to do things that are not in those individuals' best interests. The word "conman" is short for "confidence man." Bernie Madoff and Charles Ponzi are two examples of high-profile cases of misused confidence. They came across as likable and seemed to know what they were talking about, but they abused their positions for their own personal gain.

That's why demonstrating that you're trustworthy is the final follow-up to likability and confidence. When you can show your clients that they can trust you on top of having a good relationship and knowing your policies, the odds are good that you won't just win their business once—you'll keep it for a long time to come, as well.

So how do you demonstrate trustworthiness?

You can establish your trustworthiness with your immediate actions, just by living up to what you say you're going to do. In other words, what you say is golden. If you tell a client, "I'm going to call you at 2:00 p.m.," you call at 2:00 p.m. Not at 2:01 p.m., and not at 1:57 p.m. You call at 2:00 p.m. If you have a meeting at 1:00 p.m. and don't know what the traffic is like, you leave early. You make sure that you are there when you say you're going to be there.

Trustworthiness was the reason I decided to cover the misunderstanding in my client's $18,000 furniture theft policy. I saw it this way: If I said that my word was golden and that I was trustworthy, was it even possible for me to say to that client, "I'm sorry, there was a mix up and you don't have coverage?" Of course not. I could not do that and remain trustworthy. When you tell someone that you can be trusted, you have to back up your word every step of the way.

When you honor your word like this, people will start to notice that you're different. Very few people operate like this on a consistent basis. It's very rare to see a person who always does exactly what he says he's going to do, when he says he's going to do it. Living up to your word will yield tremendous benefits for you and your business in the long run.

The Character of Success

If you've achieved any degree of success in sales and have any policies under your belt right now, you've already demonstrated to some degree the three personal breakthrough qualities of likability, confidence, and trustworthiness. Take what you have and improve on it. You will be amazed at the impact that these core qualities alone have on your business.

Remember that you're not operating with the bottom line in mind. You never want to be phony about any of these qualities just to get the business. Instead, you put your focus on being genuine with each one of them. You make the decision that this is how you're going to operate, and it just happens that it will impact your income in a huge way at the same time. As your reputation grows, so will your business.

Now you're equipped with the foundation you need to create your breakthrough insurance agency. In the next chapter, I'll show you how to start growing your business without breaking the bank.

༄

Chapter 4

Breakthrough to Growth

Passing off the Paperwork

When Wendy and I started in this business, we did everything ourselves. And there was a lot to do.

I call those days "the transition period." This was before we issued policies electronically. Applications were filed on paper, with those black carbon sheets that you had to flip over to fill out the back side. I'd see customers a day before, and then I'd take mountains of paperwork with me to the fire station. Every single night, I'd be filling out paperwork until eleven o'clock, just to keep up with the administrative side of my agency.

That wasn't the lifestyle I wanted to have. I didn't want to be a slave to the paperwork. I needed help.

As soon as Wendy and I could afford it, we hired our first customer service representative.

I remember the day I passed off the paperwork. We were fantastically busy. I got two or three calls, and every one of my appointments was great: two cars and a condo, two cars and homeowners and an umbrella, then another couple cars and a homeowner policy. Everyone gave me checks.

I walked into my office with a tower of paperwork in my arms—signed applications that needed to be completed and processed. Normally, I would have taken all of that to the fire station with me and slaved over it for the next four to five hours.

Instead, I crossed over to where our new hire was waiting. I set the stack of applications on top of her desk. "I'd like you to process these, please," I said.

Then I turned around and walked out.

As I headed out the door, I thought to myself, *Yes!* I was free. And sure enough, from that day forward, my production increased. The back office was handled. All I had to focus on was production and growing the agency.

We were on our way.

The Key to Growth

Whether you're a new agent or a seasoned veteran, you're going to break through your one-person plateau pretty quickly. When that happens, you're going to need more staff. And unless you have boat-loads of money already waiting in the bank, you're going to need a system that will allow you to fund those new staff positions.

There's a right way to fund growth, and you don't have to go into debt to do it. The key to healthy growth that will keep on multiplying is simple: you have to plan, save, hire, and repeat.

A lot of people jump in without a plan. It's part of the national mentality that when money comes in, we just spend it. But if you follow that trajectory, you're going to be working for your business instead of making your business work for you. You'll be living hand to mouth, stressing over payroll, and taking out of your own salary to make overhead. If the agency hits a rough patch for a month or two, you might even have to let good people go—and then you'll have to start the process all over again.

Healthy growth involves delayed gratification. You have to plan and save before you hire and repeat. But when you do it this way, it's a whole different ball game. You come from a place of abundance instead of scarcity. You never have to worry about whether or not you'll make payroll. You have peace of mind no matter what the market looks like.

You set yourself up for success by designing your business to work for you. And that's when growth becomes effortless.

In this chapter, I'll take you through my process of funding growth in your agency and show you how to create a two-month operational account that will give you prosperity and peace of mind.

Plan, Hire, Repeat

In this business, you can create enough income through your own effort to support a basic lifestyle. There's no question about that. But you're looking for more than basic support. You're looking to move from owning your own job to owning a business. And that means bringing new people on board who can contribute and help you down that path.

To hire that first person without going into debt, you need a plan.

The Plan

Your plan is a three-step process. You need to identify the position you're looking to fill, draw a line in the sand as far as expenses, and then save to support the target goal.

Identifying the position is really getting specific about how much the position will cost. Let's say you want a new customer service representative to take on some of the paperwork. You know that you need to pay that person $15 an hour. So you do the math, and you figure out that this new hire is going to cost $2,400 a month to keep on salary.

You want to save up three months of salary for this hire before you bring the person on. That way, if for any reason the agency brings in less than expected for a month or two, you'll have plenty of money to fund the position while the new hire is acclimating.

How do you save up?

You start by drawing a line in the sand where your expenses are concerned. You look at your income and say, "I have this much money coming in right now. This is how much of it I need per month for personal and business expenses. Anything that I earn beyond this basic amount is going into the salary savings fund."

And that's it. You start saving. It helps to have online banking, so that you can transfer the money for the fund into your designated payroll savings account with the click of a button. However, regardless of your method, you have to be disciplined about it. The first savings account can take up to six months to create, and it can be tempting to break the rules when you're first starting out. But trust me, you want to get to that first hire as quickly as you can. Once you have help, your production will go up 30 to 40 percent. Put in the sweat equity and make it happen.

The Hire

As soon as you save up ninety days of salary, it's time to go out and hire that new position.

You don't use the savings account to pay the new hire. The savings is only there to subsidize in the event of an emergency. Instead, you pay the new hire with the money you were adding to the savings account every month. That money now goes directly to payroll, and you're off and running.

In the many, many times I've done this, I've found that I rarely have to depend on the savings account to pay for the position. Because as soon as that new person comes in, he or she immediately frees me up to produce more business. If the new hire is a producer, that person creates value so quickly that the savings account never loses a penny. And on the rare occasions when I have had to use the savings, I haven't used much.

But by taking this approach, you can expand your staff without stressing about going into debt or falling short of making payroll. You know that you have plenty of time and plenty of money to handle your new fixed expense.

Give Yourself a Raise

So you have your new hire and your security blanket. You're bringing this person into the business, and you're crossing your fingers that everything is going to work out. Occasionally, someone won't be a good fit and you'll have to find a replacement, but your savings account has you covered for that transition if it happens. You hire a good person, things start going well, and pretty soon you find that there's extra money coming in. Now you're completely sure that you can afford the new position every month with no shortage.

Guess what? It's time to give yourself a raise.

At my agency, we typically give ourselves a raise of 10 percent to 20 percent every time this happens. And there's no reason why this can't happen twice a year. So by taking this approach, and provided that you hire the right people and use the other systems I'll outline in the rest of this book, you can very easily give yourself a 40 percent raise in just one year.

I strongly recommend that you build automatic raises into your process like this. Finding the discipline to keep contributing to the payroll savings account can sometimes be a challenge. If that's the case, knowing that there's a raise on the near horizon will give you the motivation you need to keep at it.

Rinse and Repeat

Once you've got your new hire on board and assimilated, you don't stop there. You rinse and repeat to keep your business moving onward and upward.

Start saving for the next position you need to fill. After the first round, this usually gets easier, because you can use the funds from your last savings account to give you a head start. Maybe this time you're looking for a producer instead of a customer sales representative, and the producer makes more than the rep. You need to save $8,000 to come up with three months' salary for this position, but you already have $6,000 from the last account. All you have to do is add the $2,000 difference, and you're on your way.

When you first start saving like this, it's tough. But after a while, it becomes a habit. Before you know it, saving is second nature. And since the principle and the percentage are the same at any level, as the production numbers get bigger, so will your savings.

Keep adding the people you need to drive your growth to the next level, and keep rewarding yourself with raises as you go. This system just keeps going and going and going, and the results will amaze you.

Fund Growth Everywhere

Just as you can fund new hires using this process, you can fund everything else in your business with it, as well.

Do you need a bigger office? Draw the line in the sand, and start saving up three months' rent. Do you want to launch a new advertising campaign? Save up for it. You can grow any part of your business in big ways using this system of growth, without ever going into debt.

I'm living proof of this. At BW Baker Insurance as of 2014, we had fourteen people on staff, had doubled the square footage of our original office, had invested in new technology, and had remodeled—all without going a single dime into the red. We've never had to arrange any sort of financing to fund that growth, because everything was pre-funded prior to making the decision to go forward.

That's the power of a breakthrough growth system.

The Two-Month Operational Account

Beyond saving for individual goals, I also keep a two-month operational account.

This account is my safety net for the entire business. It holds enough to cover all my costs for two months: salaries, rents, all the expenses I have in running the agency. If a dramatic downturn happened unexpectedly, I wouldn't be caught flat-footed. And that gives me enormous peace of mind. It takes the pressure off and gives me a security factor I wouldn't have otherwise.

There's never anything wrong with saving more than you need. So if you have a stellar month now and then, put the extra into your own two-month operational account. The only thing better than prosperity is prosperity that's guaranteed to stay that way, thanks to your rainy day fund.

Out of the Picture, Into Success

I've taught this simple, effective system to hundreds of agents over the years—from novices to seasoned men and women—and all of them have seen incredible results. The more you grow your business, the less it will depend on you to stay up and running. And that's when you start to experience real success.

I remember when I started getting requests from clients to the tune of "Hi Bart, listen, could you put So-and-So on the line? I've got a new car to insure, and I'd like to talk to her." At first my reaction was, *Wait a second, what about me?* But then I caught myself. *No, no, no, wrong thought, Bart. Replace that one. This is a really good thing.*

And it was a really good thing. I went from doing everything myself to where I am today, which is focusing on generating new business and making sure that my existing clients are well taken care of. It's incredibly rare for me to take a client from beginning to end nowadays. Instead, I start the process and then hand it off. I have complete confidence in my staff and their abilities, and I trust them implicitly with the duties that I alone used to handle. That gives me a tremendous amount of freedom to keep growing the business—and to have the lifestyle I want.

That's where you're headed when you start growing your breakthrough agency with this system. And it's a great destination to keep in mind. But funding isn't the only thing that will put you on the fast track to that reality. In chapter 5, I'll teach you how to push your growth to the next level by leveraging two key players in the business: maximizers and multipliers.

❧

The 3M Breakthrough System™: Maximizers, Multipliers, and Measurement

Army of Innovators

We all live under the same time constraint of twenty-four hours in a day. But within that twenty-four hour timeframe, some of us have found a way to achieve absolutely massive success that others only dream about.

One example of this is Elon Musk. Musk was a cofounder of PayPal, the world's leading internet payment system. He could've stopped right there and been taken care of for the rest of his life— but he didn't. Instead, he went on to found Tesla Motors, the leader in electric car manufacturing. After that, he became the CEO and chief designer of SpaceX, the first privately funded company to successfully launch, orbit, and recover a spacecraft. And on top of all that he chairs SolarCity, the top provider of solar power systems in the United States.

I look at this guy and I think, *Wow, it's incredible what he's done in that period of time.* But here's the catch: he didn't do it alone.

As of 2014, Tesla Motors had a roster of ten thousand employees. SpaceX employed three thousand people, and SolarCity had over six thousand team members involved in keeping it up and running.

Elon Musk is a man with a lot of vision and mental capacity. But he never could have made all those profitable companies happen alone. He needed incredibly strong teams behind him to bring them to life.

He needed good people to help him maximize and multiply his businesses.

More Business, Less "You"

The ultimate goal with your business should be to get it to a place where it can run smoothly without you. I touched on this in the last chapter. An agency that works without depending on you is an agency that gives you the freedom you need to have the lifestyle you want.

But how do you actually make this kind of agency happen?

Like Elon Musk, you have to find a way to maximize and multiply your time. And the way you do that is by using the 3M Breakthrough System™ to build your business using maximizers, multipliers, and measurement.

Maximizers and multipliers do exactly what their titles suggest: they maximize and multiply your time, effort, and efficiency. Choosing people for your team who will be great at doing those things is important. Without maximizers and multipliers on your agency roster, you'll hit a ceiling. There will always be a limit to how much business you can do in a set amount of time. But when you bring these team members into your agency, time becomes limitless. If you need more of it, you just hire more maximizers and multipliers, ad infinitum.

And the more time and people you have on your side, the more your business can grow.

The third M, measurement, pulls it all together. It's not enough to have a system and work hard. Without consistent new premium coming in, your business won't thrive. Everything we do is based on keeping what we have while adding to it. Measurement lets you know if you are on track.

In this chapter, I'll teach you the role of great maximizers and multipliers and show you how to ensure efficiency in your agency by measuring progress.

Maximizers

What is a maximizer?

A maximizer is somebody who allows you to focus a full 80 percent of your time on building relationships and creating income for the business, while only 20 percent of it goes toward the administrative duties of owning an agency. Your maximizer handles almost all of the technical issues of your job for you, making sure that all your systems run smoothly and correctly on the back end. And in doing that, your maximizer literally maximizes the time you have to build wealth for your breakthrough insurance agency.

Maximizers are the first positions you should be looking to hire, if you're a new agent. They're your customer service representatives and administrative assistants, and they play a key role in the 3M Breakthrough System™. You need them to free your hands from technical processes like paperwork so that you can focus on generating new sources of income. When you can maximize the time you spend on bringing in business, you position yourself to become a very effective entrepreneur.

After you have your maximizers in place, you're ready to add the next key players to your team: multipliers.

Multipliers

A multiplier is an individual who creates relationships and brings in income.

When you first start your agency, you yourself are the lone multiplier in your business. But as I mentioned, you're going to reach a point in your growth where your one-man shop just isn't cutting it anymore. You only have so much time in a day. Even if you're very efficient, have high-end clients, and get a lot of referrals, you're still going to hit that ceiling where you effectively "have a job." It's a high-end job, but it's a job nonetheless. You can't pull yourself out of the equation and still expect to bring in income.

When that time comes, your question will be, "How am I going to continue to grow this business?" And your answer, using the 3M Breakthrough System™, will be, "By getting more multipliers."

Your multipliers will do exactly what you yourself are doing in your agency: they'll build great relationships and create more income.

Now, you may be thinking: But Bart, you said that this was going to be a referral-based agency. How do the multipliers generate new business if they're not going on the offense and making outside sales?

It's true that most of your business will eventually be based on referrals, as I'll explain in more detail later. But even when that's the case, your multipliers will still be able to generate new business—often from the clients you already have.

One example is policy reviews. At my agency, we do annual client reviews where we conduct reviews of the customer's existing policies, identify gaps in the coverage using my Gap Elimination Process™, and then reach out to the client with additional insurance policies to fill those gaps.

There's a bigger need for this than you might think. For example, say somebody moves into the area and is referred to you for a home-owner policy. They need that policy taken care of quickly because escrow is closing soon, so that was all they ended up doing at the time.

Well, later, one of our multipliers will do a review with that client and say, "You know, you're at risk for all these other things," and a lot of the time we'll end up writing additional lines of business for auto insurance, umbrella coverage, life insurance, and anything else they need. The multiplier is the one who finds those opportunities. He or she is also the one who fields your referral leads and closes them.

So your multipliers aren't going to sit around twiddling their thumbs. On the contrary, you have to keep in mind that they're going to be in the same position that you were in: the time they have to generate more business is going to depend on how many technical tasks they're responsible for. And that means you need to pair your multipliers with maximizers as fast as you possibly can. Once you put the two of them together, they're unstoppable—and they will do incredible things for your business.

How to Choose Great Maximizers and Multipliers

You might think that the majority of multipliers are Type-A go-getters while most maximizers are detail-oriented introverts. But that's not the case. I've found that many of the same qualities make maximizers and multipliers successful in this business.

The first one is likability. I covered the importance of this for you personally in chapter 3, but it should also be a key quality in your team members. One of the comments I get most from customers is, "Everybody in your office is so nice." And that's what you're looking for, because you can't teach "nice." Choose people for your team whom you can treat well, so that they in turn will treat your clients well.

After likability, there are a couple of other traits that great maximizers and multipliers have in common. I identify them using the Kolbe Index (www.kolbe.com), an assessment that analyzes how people work. Kolbe looks at four areas: fact finder, follow through, quick start, and implementer. A high fact-finder score means that someone is very detail oriented and structured in the way he or she does things. High follow through indicates someone who is stable, timely, and reliable. Quick start is someone who has lots of ideas and can jump from concept to concept quickly, and an implementer is someone who makes things happen on a physical level.

I've found that the best maximizers and multipliers are people who have high fact-finder and follow-through scores in the Kolbe Index. They're detail oriented and good at following up over time. They're not flashy, aggressive, go-for-it type of people—even the ones who bring in new business. That's because my model of running the agency is not to "sell" people. My model is to build relationships and give good advice. The people in my office sell a ton of insurance, because they don't come across as salesy. They come across as likable and competent.

In fact, my maximizers often become my multipliers. Someone comes in to fill a maximizer role, like a customer sales rep, and once that person gets good at what he or she does, you move them up as the next natural step. Then you find another maximizer to support your new multiplier.

Now, this doesn't mean everyone on your team has to be a fact finder or a follow through-er. However, if you do bring on people from the other categories, it's a good idea to pair them with supporters who have fact-finder and follow-through qualities.

I personally scored highest in the quick-start category, and it's really true that I can hop from idea to idea and forget what I was doing last week. So I have a personal assistant who is great with follow through. Her name is Vanessa, and she follows through with things that I don't even remember that she's doing anymore. She reminds me of the things I overlook, and that allows me to keep growing the business. It's a win-win combination.

When it comes to finding good maximizers and multipliers, it's not rocket science. Hire people who are likable, who will follow through with what they say they're going to do, and who will represent you well. That's all you really need.

Measure Up

Once you have great maximizers and multipliers, you're in a prime position to fuel new growth in your business. But before you can really make that happen, you have to add the third M to the 3M Breakthrough System™: measurement.

It's not enough to bring somebody into the agency, tell them what their job description is, and then say, "Go get 'em, tiger!" You need to have a system of measurement in place to determine whether that individual is successful in terms of gross written premium, retention, and policies in force (PIF). Even more importantly, you need to clearly define what success means to the company in those areas so that everybody on your team knows what it looks like and how they're doing.

When it comes to determining the benchmarks you're going to measure, I go by this rule: if it feels a little scary, yet you feel that you can do it, then that's a great number. The worst thing you can do is settle for mediocrity. You don't want to set outrageous goals, but at the same time you never want to say, "Well, you know, maybe that's a little too high for comfort." If you do that, you'll never reach your full potential.

In our agency, the way we define success is with a monthly monetary production goal. As of 2015, the figure we used was $80,000 each of new business coming in from our personal and commercial departments. And we do it old school: we put a big thermometer on the wall with $80,000 at the top and $0 at the bottom. Then we just keep track of how much business is coming in on a weekly basis. And at the end of the month, we celebrate our success by doing something nice for the office, like taking everyone out to a nice dinner.

We don't always hit the $80,000 mark. It's a big number, and some months are better than others. But the team knows that if we did it once we can do it again, and everybody is aware of what the monthly tally is all the time. The number is something we aspire to, and because of that we find a way to make it work.

What you measure improves, and what you measure and report improves exponentially. That's the power of measurement at its best.

A New Equation

Once you start populating your team with maximizers and multipliers according to the 3M Breakthrough System™, you really begin to duplicate your efforts. The responsibilities that used to fall solely on your shoulders are now shared concerns. Eventually, you can take yourself out of the production equation altogether and assume the new role of supporting your team. That's an incredible transition, because your business is no longer all about you doing everything yourself.

You're well on your way to a business that works for you—and the freedom and lifestyle that come along with it.

But your breakthrough insurance agency isn't done yet. In addition to great people, you need an edge that will differentiate you from your competition. That edge is the Gap Elimination Process™, and in the next chapter I'll take you through the ins and outs of it.

Chapter 6

The Gap Elimination Process™

Remember the Remodel

A very successful couple in their late fifties came into my office one day for their annual coverage review. We were going through their policies top to bottom like I always do, and everything was fine—until we got to the home insurance.

"Okay, so your house is three thousand square feet, insured for $900,000. That's about $300 per square foot," I said. "How do you feel about that?"

For a long moment, both of them just stared at me. Then the husband said, "We remodeled our house."

"Oh, all right," I replied. "What did you do?"

"The house is now five thousand square feet," he told me. "We spent almost $2 million on the remodel."

I blinked. "That's . . . that's kind of important to fill me in about, you know."

"Oh my god, we know," his wife was shaking her head. "It's just that we had so much going on during that whole process. I can't believe we didn't even think about the insurance!"

"Okay," I said, "we'll get it sorted out. That's why we do this review process. How long has it been since you remodeled the house?"

It turned out that they'd been living that way for over a year—with $900,000 of coverage for a home that should have been insured for about $2.9 million.

I don't normally do pricing and signups on the spot, but that day I broke my own cardinal rule. I believe in Murphy's Law, and I didn't want them to go through one more night with that kind of liability hanging over their heads. If you uncover a risk that big, you've got to fix it—right then and there.

So I brought in someone from Personal Lines, and we figured out the numbers. I got a rate; the couple agreed to it. The transaction happened immediately. And they walked out of my office that day a lot safer than when they walked in.

The Gap Elimination Process™

Gaps in coverage happen more often than many individuals think. It's our job, as good insurance people, to uncover those gaps and eliminate them. For this, I use a system I designed called the Gap Elimination Process™ (GEP).

The Gap Elimination Process™ is a comprehensive review of coverage. This isn't just any review. It's the backbone of your agency. When a customer comes on board, you make a promise to that person that you're going to keep their assets safe by making sure they stay properly covered. The GEP is your fulfillment of that promise

I call the GEP a "process" because it's not something you do once and then that's it, you're done. It's a process because it never ends. You'll do it today, you'll do it next year, and you'll keep doing it as long as you have that client, because it's your job to make sure that that person's coverage remains current.

And the client isn't the only one who benefits from the Gap Elimination Process™. The GEP benefits your breakthrough insurance agency as well. This system will dramatically improve your retention rate, add additional lines of business to your books, allow you to target specific lines of business that you would like to grow, and create an agency that increases referrals on a daily basis.

It will be your unique edge over your competition—and a major tool in pushing your success to the "breakthrough" levels you're looking for.

The Gap Elimination Process™ is unique because of the level of detail it entails and the post-review process it follows to actually enforce the suggestions for coverage. In this chapter, I'll cover how the GEP works, teach you how to engage your customers in a discussion, and show you how finding discounts for your clients can translate into lifelong business.

The GEP Approach

You always want to offer your clients regular Gap Elimination Process™ reviews. By "regular," I mean annual. These reviews are like checkups. They're designed to make sure that no gaps of coverage have occurred over the previous year and that the client is still getting the best possible pricing on his or her policies.

I can tell you from experience that the new business you'll bring in from annual reviews will definitely make them worth your while, financially. A full 20 percent of our business comes from reviewing our clients' existing insurance coverage and fulfilling new needs, when appropriate.

Annual reviews also increase retention. Many agencies out there just sell the policy, take the customer's money, and are never heard from again. The retention level of those agencies is typically very low, because they don't create any value as far as a relationship with the customer. Offering regular reviews is a form of outreach. In fact, a J.D. Power study showed that even if customers don't take advantage of the review, the fact that you offer one positively impacts their willingness to stay with your agency.

So how do you approach your clients for their annual GEP review?

The process starts with sending a letter. But not just any letter. I've always been surprised by the number of people who pass on the opportunity to review their coverage. They look at it like having to go to the dentist. For a long time, only four or five customers out of one hundred responded to our offer of a review—about 4 percent or 5 percent. Then, in 2013, we found a new way to write the letter that met with some really good results.

Instead of an ordinary reminder notice about the review, the letter gave our customers four options to choose how they wanted to handle it. Option one was to schedule a traditional in-person review. Option two was to schedule a phone review. The third option was for me to send my coverage update recommendations to the client, followed by a call or meeting to go over the suggestions. The last option was to do nothing, and next to that one we wrote "not recommended" in parentheses.

This new approach with the letter bumped up our response rate to about 15 percent. Most people chose the third option, because it seemed like the least hassle on their part. And that was fine; it got the conversation started. You can use this approach to connect with clients who might not otherwise see the need.

As I said, we offer reviews once a year, and we have a specific A-to-Z process that allows us to cover everyone in our database over the course of twelve months. I cover this and many other approach techniques in my workshops. To learn more about the workshops, you can visit my website, www.bwbaker.com.

The GEP Review

Once you've successfully approached your client, you have a green light to conduct your Gap Elimination Process™ review. This is when you'll have the opportunity to put the GEP system to work for you and your customer by reviewing every aspect of their coverage in detail and identifying areas where they may be at risk.

You always want to start off the review itself with niceties. This is important because it rekindles the relationship. To give you an idea of how valuable it is, I spend the first ten minutes of a thirty-five to forty-minute review just reconnecting with the client like this.

After that bond has been reestablished, you're ready to get down to business. And there are two things you want to do right off the bat: explain the Gap Elimination Process™ and position yourself to bring up policies that you may not currently service.

I explain the GEP like this: "We have a system of review for your insurance that we call the Gap Elimination Process, and this is how it works. We just want to make sure that there are no gaps in your coverage, that you're properly insured, and that you're getting all the discounts that you qualify for."

Then I follow that explanation up with my positioning statement. I learned this statement from Bill Elliot, who used to run a major financial services firm. It takes a little practice to make it your own, but the time involved is well worth the effort. It goes like this:

"In order to properly do our risk review today, we'll look at all your policies and make sure the goals you had when you took them out still apply. Things have a way of changing. This will include your life insurance, long-term care, and disability policies. Whatever we don't have today, my assistant can follow up with and get copies of to complete the process later. Lastly, we'll make sure the policies are still as efficient as they can be from a cost standpoint and that they feature all the benefits that are currently available. Does that make sense?"

The client never says, "No, that doesn't make sense. I don't want to be properly insured or have the best price." They always say, "Yes, that makes sense."

Now, you've positioned yourself to get a look at all of that customer's policies that you don't currently have yourself. You can tell your client, "That's great. Anything we don't have for our review today, I'll have my assistant follow up with you to get copies of those policies so we can have a conversation about them later."

We've written a ton of additional business at my agency because of this positioning statement alone. Oftentimes, people had their other policies written by agents who never checked in again, so those policies have become obsolete—they don't have the latest endorsements. When that happens, we're able to transfer that coverage within our fold to be of service.

After you've given your positioning statement, you move forward with the rest of the review—home insurance, auto insurance, umbrella, life, disability, and anything else that the client may have. The thing to keep in mind for this is that you want to engage the client. You don't want to drone on forever and put them to sleep. Cover everything, but be short and sweet about it, and explain things using real-world scenarios whenever you can.

When you do come across something that needs to be discussed, bring it up as a question instead of dictating what you think the limits should be. "So it looks like your home is currently insured for $300 per square foot," you can say. "How do you feel about that?"

Most of the time the client will respond, "Well, I don't know. What's your opinion?" That's when you can say, if warranted, "Well, based on my experience and the size of your home, you may want to consider basing it around $400 a square foot instead." The figure you recommend will vary depending on the value of the house. The client will ask you how much it costs to upgrade, and you give them a ballpark estimate and then say, "I'll get you a quote." You don't want to go through the full process right there, or the meeting will last three hours—something neither you nor your client will appreciate.

With the GEP, one contact typically leads to another contact, which leads to another contact. It creates a constant flow of business to have this process and go through the different types of coverage on a regular basis. Just review everything, and the odds are good that you'll be glad you did.

For details of what the Gap Elimination Process™ actually encompasses, read my first book, *If an Elephant Sits on You, Are You Covered?* I also cover the fine points of the GEP in my workshops.

The GEP Follow-Up

The last key step in the Gap Elimination Process™ is the follow-up. This is an important differentiator of the GEP system, because the vast majority of agencies out there tell the client right there on the spot what his or her options are, and that's the end of it. They lose a lot of business that way, and their clients remain at risk.

We do things differently with the GEP. At the end of the review, we tell our clients, "We're going to memorialize this conversation. I'll send out a post-review letter that just reiterates what we discussed and what the prices are for those items that you're interested in. Then we'll follow up and get your decision about what you want to do."

So we mail out that letter, and send an email copy of it as well. We make it very clean and simple, with bullet points and red highlights for the things we're suggesting. Then we schedule the follow-up, and the conversation goes quickly. "Yes on this, no on that," and we're done.

I find that customers love this way of doing things. They feel that their needs have been well addressed, that we've communicated with them well, and that we're on top of things. They're happy, and we keep their business for a long time.

Don't Discount the Discounts

Something you want to keep in mind when you're going through the Gap Elimination Process™ with your customers is not to overlook the discounts. You always want to make sure that the client is getting the best price they can possibly get. First, because it's the right thing to do, and second, people definitely remember that. "You know when I saw Bart?" they'll say. "I had my review and he got my price down. There were all these areas where I can now get a better rate."

Finding discounts is a very valuable way to solidify your relationship with a client, because it lets the person know that you really are looking out for his or her best interest. So know the current discounts that carriers offer. Is your client a doctor, policeman, nurse, or scientist? Can they get a discount for having their home and auto insurance with the same carrier? Are they being surcharged for things that no longer apply, like youthful driver rates after their kids have already moved out of the house?

Ask the right questions, and get your clients the best coverage they can have for the lowest price. When they see that you are taking care of business and minding the shop, it will do amazing things for your retention at the end of the day.

Close the Gap

The Gap Elimination Process™ is something I created in order to have a comprehensive, easy-to-follow system that captures all of the outside business from clients and memorializes the conversations and suggestions we cover with those individuals. In my workshop, you can become certified and licensed to use my GEP system and to post my GEP whiteboard video on your website.

Individuals at any income level will have gaps of coverage that you can uncover when you conduct annual reviews—and a lot of discounts that can be applied to their policies that they didn't have before. Always keep in mind that the thought process with these isn't just to squeeze more premium out of your customers. In fact, the idea behind them isn't anything like that whatsoever.

The goal is to genuinely insure your clients correctly while making sure that they have the best pricing they can possibly have. When you go into it with that mindset, the client feels it. People are intuitive. They know when you respect them, and they know when they're being taken advantage of. I never care whether I make the sale or not. I just want my customers to have the best coverage they can get with my guidance, if they want it. And because I go into it with that intention, it so happens that my business thrives. Yours will, too.

꙳

"It had long since come to my attention that people of accomplishment rarely sat back and let things happen to them. They went out and happened to things.

—LEONARDO DA VINCI

Chapter 7

The Six Breakthrough Departments

Organic Growth

My business has always grown organically, with one department giving rise to the next.

It's a lot like a banyan tree. The tree begins small, with just one trunk. As it grows, its branches expand until it starts to drop aerial roots. Those roots burrow into the ground, and after a while they turn into new tree trunks. They're still related to the main tree, but they really support themselves.

We see this everywhere in nature. When children are born, they are completely dependent upon their parents. Then as they grow up, they become self-sufficient. They're still part of the family structure. Yet they have enough self-sufficiency to keep their own lives up and running.

Our insurance agency has grown like this from the very beginning. When we started out, our organization chart had one word at the top of it: "Agency." Wendy and I were all of our departments. Then, as we became more stable financially, we brought on maximizers and multipliers to help.

In time, those team members took on more and more responsibility. They started running different departments in the agency, and they were able to financially exist on their own. Not only were they able to pay their own salaries, they actually started to create a profit. Production climbed faster than ever—and then it just kept climbing, and more and more departments formed.

That's the power of organic growth in your business.

The Specialization Secret

When you first start an insurance agency, you yourself are every department in the business. Personal and commercial, life and health, financial services—all of it is dependent on you to function. In earlier chapters, I've shown you how to start moving away from that model by growing your business with maximizers and multipliers. But there's one more thing you need to do before you can really free yourself from the day-to-day operations of your agency: build specialized departments.

As I learned from Troy Korsgaden, specialization is key to making the breakthrough insurance agency model work. You need to create specialized departments and fill those departments with maximizers and multipliers who specialize in those exact types of insurance. The only other alternative is to go the "mini-me" route, where you train one person to do everything that you can do, and that's a bad idea for a whole host of reasons. "Mini-me's" are hard to find and hard to train, and if they move on, their loss is devastating for the business.

Compare that to specializing. Hiring for a narrower job description in a specialized department is much easier than trying to find a jack of all trades. Training goes faster because you only have to teach the person about one kind of insurance, so it's dramatically easier to get that position up and running. And if the individual leaves, he or she will be much easier to replace than the "mini-me" employee.

The more you promote specialized departments, the faster you can replace your operational roles in the business. And the faster you replace yourself, the more freedom you'll have to keep growing the agency—and to have the kind of lifestyle you want.

Now, don't mistake my meaning here: as an agency, you do need to offer everything. The agency as a whole should not specialize in one type of insurance, because it just makes sense to offer all possible solutions to your clients instead of having to refer them out to somebody else. There's no reason to let the income potential from another line of business pass you by. You want to set things up so that your specialized departments can refer business to one another. But within the departments themselves, specializing will make you stronger and more efficient.

This chapter will walk you through the six departments of a breakthrough insurance agency, show you how to structure them, and give you guidelines on hiring the right people to fill those specialized departments once you design them.

The Six Breakthrough Departments

Your breakthrough agency should have six specialized customer-facing departments: personal lines, commercial lines, life and health, front office and claims concierge, financial services, and marketing.

Personal Lines

Your personal lines department includes types of insurance related to personal exposure, such as auto, home, and umbrella coverage. It also includes scheduled items like jewelry and fine art, as well as earthquake and flood coverage. The reason you group all of these together under "personal lines" instead of putting them into smaller individual departments is that you want your client to have one point of contact for most of his or her needs.

For example, if George calls us up and says he needs all the basic types of insurance, we're not going to have him talk to Sally about his home insurance, Joe about his auto insurance, and Chris about his umbrella insurance. We want one individual to communicate with George for all of those things. Not only does George receive a better experience, but we have the chance to build a relationship with him—and that helps us retain his business.

Commercial Lines

Your commercial lines department follows the same concept as personal lines, only with kinds of insurance that have to do with commercial exposure. For example, a client might own commercial real estate, like apartment buildings or shopping centers. Or an individual might own a business of his or her own, such as a dentist's office or a manufacturing company.

As with personal lines, you want to keep the different types of commercial coverage together in one department to simplify the process for the client. The individual only has to talk to one person to make sure that all of his or her commercial insurance needs are met. It's easier on everyone, and it's one more way to build good relationships.

We typically get most of our commercial clients through their personal lines policies. When someone comes in for home or auto insurance, we build upon our relationship with that person. Later, we come to find that they have commercial exposure, and since they've come to trust us with their personal lines, they give us the opportunity to cover their commercial assets, too. You don't have to do it this way. But this is a model that has worked really well for us.

Life and Health

The life and health department functions similarly to personal and commercial lines. In addition to the policies that it produces itself, this department is responsible for the administrative side of issuing any life insurance that is sold by the personal and commercial lines departments. The life and health department gets a ton of referrals internally, as well as from our customers. Health insurance is obviously one of those products that everyone needs. When clients are able to purchase from, and be serviced by, an agency that they already know, it's a big win for everyone. This department handles individual and group health, Medicare supplements, long-term care, and disability insurance.

I am always surprised when I hear of agencies that don't sell health insurance. They say that they make more from other types of insurance, and that may be true. But they are still leaving valuable commission dollars on the table that could be used to fund the growth of their agencies.

When you staff your life and health department using the 3M Breakthrough System™ from chapter 5 and fuel it with the referral system I'll talk about in chapter 9, this department can add serious revenue to your breakthrough insurance agency.

Front Office and Claims Concierge

The front office department is like a catchall for the rest of the agency. It typically takes care of the first point of contact, especially for telephones. However, when the other departments are completely backed up, the front office picks up the slack. It also handles everything that falls outside of the other departments, like clients who call in with policy inquiries or who need to make payments.

Beyond all that, the front office is our claims concierge, also known as "Claims Central." We don't give our customers an 800 telephone number and say, "This is the number you have to call regarding your claim." We handle it for them. We consider that a value proposition that they purchased when they decided to do business with us: we're going to be their point of contact and guide them through the claims process. Our claims concierge takes their information, files their claim, and generally facilitates communication between the client and the claims office.

For example, say someone is in a car accident. All that person has to do is call the claims concierge, and we file the claim, arrange for the body shop, take care of the car rental, and do all the follow up.

If anything ever comes up, the clients know that they have a friendly person waiting to help them in the front office.

Financial Services

The financial services department can encompass a lot of things, such as mutual funds, retirement accounts, IRAs, 401(k)s, 529 college savings plans, and annuities that are tied to the stock market.

I know some agencies that do not offer financial services and other agencies that just dabble in it. I also know many agencies that do a fantastic job with financial services and have close to $100 million worth of customers' assets under management. I truly believe that the breakthrough insurance agency of the future is one that focuses on financial services as much as it does all the other types of insurance. Why? Because an agency with a financial services department is able to take care of all of a client's needs. It's part of the philosophy of building a strong business: you want to manage and control absolutely every aspect of the insurance transactions that happen, because that puts you in control. The more control you have, the better you can serve your customers.

We're not looking to be Merrill Lynch here. If somebody has a huge $50 million financial services portfolio, that person probably wouldn't be best served by the kind of financial services department I'm describing. The idea is that we're looking to be able to offer financial services to clients who want to consolidate. Who better to have that conversation with than the agency that has been taking care of their other potential risk exposures? It's just one more opportunity to improve efficiency, so the client doesn't have to reach out to multiple sources.

Insurance is getting much broader than just handling people's property and casualty exposure. When you add a financial services department to the equation, you position yourself as the point of contact for everything your client needs.

Marketing

Finally, the sixth department in a breakthrough insurance agency is marketing.

Ultimately, your goal should be to create a referral-based agency, and I'll explain that more in chapter 9. However, even after you reach the point where your business is 80 percent to 90 percent referrals, you should always keep some type of marketing happening on a consistent basis, just to funnel in new business and smooth out any bumps in the road.

Marketing is important because it always puts you in front of new people. And you need new people to come in; they're part of your life-blood—especially when you're starting out. That's why you always want to keep your hand on the pulse of the market, and for that you need a marketing arm.

Our marketing department consists of an individual who conducts marketing for all of the departments in our agency: personal lines, commercial lines, life and health, and financial services. We don't need a different marketing person for each one of those departments. Instead, the marketing department focuses on whatever area makes the most sense at a particular time.

For example, under the Affordable Care Act, you have an open enrollment period for health insurance. That enrollment period runs from November through January. If you wanted to increase your book of health insurance, you would have your marketing department focus on that leading up to and during the enrollment period. Once the enrollment period ends, you start marketing for other things.

Whatever you're looking to grow in your agency, just focus your marketing activity in that direction. Letters and follow-ups, target advertising in magazines and newspapers, social media, online marketing—all of these are tools at your disposal. Whatever happens to work in your area, give it to your marketing department and let them get it done.

Department Setup and Support

Now you know the six key departments in a breakthrough in-surance agency. But how do you go about actually setting them up?

The great thing is that you can use the same system for this that you used earlier for bringing on new people. Identify the department you want to create, save the resources to make it happen, and then start building it up with maximizers and multipliers who specialize in that line of insurance.

Keep track of the growth of your different departments with an organization chart. Write out the six key departments, and identify the positions you need to support each of them. In the beginning, your name is going to be on every line of the chart. Your goal is to replace your name with new ones as your business expands, and the organization chart is a great way to track your progress.

As your departments grow, you shift into the role of supporter. You do as little as possible of the actual operations in the actual departments themselves, but that doesn't mean you drop them completely. The departments aren't islands, and you can't expect them to go out into the cold world without you and just expect them to make things happen.

As the agency owner, you give your people all the support they need to make their lives easier, using the 3M Breakthrough System™ discussed in chapter 5. You spoon-feed the business as much as you can. And that gives you a thriving, breakthrough agency.

Fill Your Departments

Now that you have your department structure set up, you need a strategy to hire the right people and slot them into the specialized departments within your business.

There's actually a right way to do this. When I was starting out, I had a hard time hiring good people. We had to go through our share of employees who were dishonest, tardy, and lacking a strong work ethic. But the silver lining to those mistakes is that we've learned how to hire good people.

Just like everything else in your agency, you want to set things up so that the hiring process pretty much works without you. In the beginning, of course, you're going to be talking to people yourself. But once your specialized departments are up and running, you pass the initial work off to the department supervisor, who is a multiplier. Your supervisor does the initial interview. If the candidate passes that first test, the supervisor sends the individual on to a second interview with human resources.

As the owner of the agency, you only get involved at the final stage—the third interview—to give your final approval of the new hire. At that stage, you let the person know that you're very interested in hiring them, and you give them the Kolbe Index test I talked about in chapter 5. If the Kolbe assessment comes back looking the way you want it and your intuition gives you a good feeling about the candidate, you make them an offer and bring them on board.

In my agency, we put all of our new hires on a thirty-day probationary period to see whether or not they're going to be a good fit.

Some people say that ninety days is the ideal for this. However, I find that you can get a pretty darn good indication of where things are heading with someone by the thirty-day mark. I've had a few situations in the past where we've taken a new hire through the whole ninety days even though I knew at day thirty that the individual was not someone I wanted to move forward with, and I lost the money, time, and energy that went into those additional sixty days of keeping that person on the roster.

An agent I know has a great expression: "Slow to hire, quick to fire." I think there's a lot of truth to that idea. If you think someone could still have potential at the thirty-day mark, take them all the way to ninety days. But if you know at day thirty that the person isn't going to fit the bill, let them go, and get on with finding the individual you need.

The Importance of Good People

I touched on this in chapter 5, but it bears repeating: you really can't overvalue the importance of good people. Your staff members are your voice to the customers, and that makes them a direct reflection of you as the figurehead of the agency. That means that the same qualities of likability, confidence, and trustworthiness that you're building in yourself need to be present in the people you hire.

So if you are faced with the choice of two candidates—someone who is inexpensive and someone who costs more but is obviously a person of better character—my advice is to go with the individual who has the personal qualities you're looking for. Don't be lulled into the decision based on cost alone. I've always found that it's better to pay a little bit more, even if I really don't want to, because the long-term results were exactly what I needed: better production, better retention, and better quality to the agency.

The Structure of Success

Setting up your departments is an incredibly gratifying process. You'll see and appreciate the production they bring to your agency, and you'll know that they came from strong roots, because you truly did build them—one department at a time.

I'll say it again: the byproduct of having specialized departments in place is *freedom*. When you're no longer worrying about wearing all the hats yourself, you can put your focus on growing the business. You're still the conductor of the orchestra in that you still support your departments. But now your main job description is to drive the vision for the agency and find ways to make it bigger and better going forward.

And that's exactly where you want to be.

Once your departments are in place, the underlying structure of your breakthrough insurance agency is in solid shape. The next thing you need to look at is the fine-tuning. I'll take you through the nuts and bolts of that in chapter 8.

ᏅᎦᎦᏅ

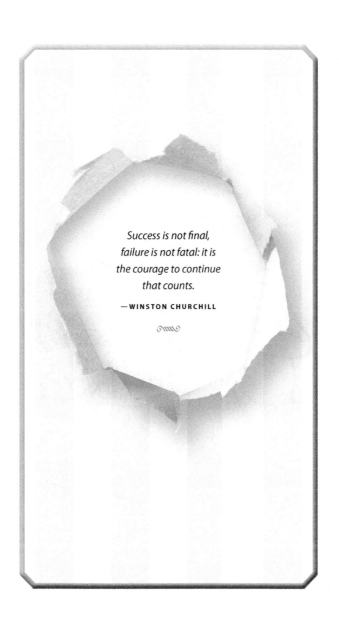

Success is not final,
failure is not fatal: it is
the courage to continue
that counts.

—WINSTON CHURCHILL

Chapter 8

Fine-Tuning Your Breakthrough Agency

Don't Hold the Phone

One day in 2014, a mentor of mine and I were talking, and we decided to make plans to get together with our wives and go out to dinner.

"Hey listen, Bart, I'll give you a call at the office and we'll figure out when and where we're going to meet," my mentor said. His name is A.C. Warnack, and he's a tremendous individual with great integrity and business acumen. I have a lot of respect for him.

"Okay, great," I agreed.

So a while later, I got a call from him at my office. I picked up the phone, and the first thing he said to me was, "If anybody in my office answered the phone the way that your receptionist just did for me, I'd fire her."

Oh my god, I thought, *what did she do?* "What happened?" I asked him.

It turned out that when A.C. had called and asked to speak with me, the receptionist had responded, "Do you mind if I ask what it's regarding?" A.C. took offense to that.

"I said, 'Honey, I'll tell you what it's regarding. It's regarding I want to talk to Bart,'" he told me. "In my business, any person who calls and asks for anybody—including me as the president—gets put through. They don't get the third degree. They don't get cleared to see if it's somebody worthy of having a conversation with the person they're calling for. They just get transferred."

It sounded to me like A.C.'s method would create a lot of extra work for most people. But I respected him so much that I decided I would try it. *I'll give it a shot as a test,* I thought, *just to see how it goes.*

And I implemented that process. I got my staff together and announced, "Okay, from now on, any phone calls that come in are to be put straight through. We're not going to ask what it's regarding or any of that. Just pick up the phone, get the name, and serve the call."

I noticed a change in the response we got from our clients immediately.

First they were surprised at how quickly their call went through—and that initial moment of surprise quickly turned to appreciation. A lot of my clients are businesspeople. They're busy, and they appreciate that they get to bypass the delay when they're trying to get ahold of me, or anyone else in my office. They immediately detected that we do business differently at my agency, and that has literally led to more business for us.

As small as it sounds, A.C.'s direct-transfer phone method became a differentiator in our agency. And we continue to see great results from it to this day.

Your Breakthrough Advantage

It really doesn't matter how long you're in business, whether you're talking about one year or thirty years. You constantly have to fine-tune both your business and yourself. And the way you fine-tune is by finding breakthrough advantages that give you an edge over your competition.

My business coach, Dan Sullivan, calls this concept "creating an unfair advantage." An unfair advantage is a way of doing business that your competition cannot copy and, in most cases, doesn't comprehend. It causes a shift in the client's perception of doing business with you because of something that you have done. In an insurance agency, that often amounts to implementing systems and processes that are unique to you—systems that your competition cannot understand or duplicate.

A.C.'s method of answering phones is a great example of this. It gives us an edge over the big companies out there, like Geico and Progressive. You're never going to be able to call one of those companies and say, "Hi, may I talk to Kim, please? She helped me last time." Even if Geico and Progressive understand the concept of building personal relationships, they can't implement it—and that's when our method of personalized service becomes an unfair advantage.

When you have an unfair advantage that fits the market you are going after, you will see a significant increase in the speed of business. Your referrals will go up, and your ability to expand your targeted market will improve. Without an unfair advantage, growth will happen more slowly, and it will be more of an uphill battle.

This chapter will take you through the different ways you can find your unique breakthrough advantage, from identifying a niche to leveraging several tools of the fine-tuning trade.

Know Your Niche

To go big, you really need to go small. And by that, I mean it's really important to find your niche.

Having a niche doesn't mean you only offer one type of insurance. It means you target one specific section of the market. Once you're in the door with that piece of the market, it will bring you business for all of your insurance lines through referral and association.

For example, one good friend of mine sells insurance to a niche of homeowner associations. That's all he does. But boy, does he write a lot of insurance for those associations. And after that niche gets him over the threshold, guess what? He also writes insurance for all of the homeowners in those associations—people who need auto, umbrella, health coverage, and everything else.

His target niche naturally leads him to other business.

The same thing happens in my agency. My niche is individuals in the higher end of the marketplace with nicer homes. The people I target come to me for homeowner insurance and other personal lines, at first. But as we build the relationship, I come to find they have other properties and investments. And because they like me and have confidence in my knowledge, before long they want me to look at their commercial insurance, too.

I don't target commercial insurance as my niche market. But that department of my agency thrives because of the niche I *do* focus on. You don't necessarily need to target the higher end of your market-place, though that can often be a wise move, since those individuals usually have more to insure. At the end of the day, how you get in doesn't matter, as long as you're strategic and find a way to get in somewhere. Once you do that, your business grows itself.

When you first start out, you may not know what your niche is. You'll probably have to try on a lot of different hats before you find the one that fits you best, and that's okay. Do whatever it takes to get your feet on the ground. Leverage whatever prior experience you have to give yourself a head start. And as soon as you discover an area that you feel really comfortable doing business in—as soon as that niche becomes apparent—take it.

The sooner you identify your niche, the sooner you'll be able to tailor your business for that audience—and the faster you'll gain your breakthrough advantage in the market.

Tools of the Fine-Tuning Trade

A strong niche gives you an enormous edge in the business. But it's only the beginning of building your unfair advantage. Here are a few tools you can use to keep fine-tuning your breakthrough insurance agency.

Write a Book

Writing a book is a great way to create an unfair advantage, because it gives you a ton of instant credibility.

I've found this to be true, personally. In 2013, I published my first book, *If an Elephant Sits on You, Are You Covered?* I now give that out to prospective clients when I meet them. "Hi, how are you?" I'll say. "It's nice to meet you. I'd like to give you a copy of my latest book on how to be properly insured."

And that immediately takes the conversation up to a whole different level. The fact that I have a book positions me as an expert in the industry in the client's eye. It gives me an unfair advantage over another agent who could have the same conversation with this client, but doesn't have the book. Because I'm the one with the book, I'm perceived differently by the customer.

If you're not a writer, there are editors out there who can help you create your book. I've always believed that quality pays in the long run, so for my book I chose to go with a professional editing services company, Author Bridge Media. But there are other ways to make a book happen that cost less, and that will also jumpstart your credibility with a breakthrough advantage.

Keep a Blog

Another way to create an unfair advantage is to keep a blog. You can start your own blog about insurance, publish it, and promote it.

I know a Realtor in Malibu who has created a great edge for his business by doing this. His name is Michael Gardner, and he happens to be a client of mine. Michael runs an excellent blog about real estate, and he's told me that he's brought in a lot of business from people who found him through that blog. Whenever you're searching for property in Malibu, he pops up.

Contribute to your blog on a regular basis. Keep it interesting and informative. Blogs are effective, and they can be a very simple way to create a breakthrough advantage for you and your agency.

Do Internet Radio

Another thing you can do to create your competitive edge is become a radio host.

Now, I'm obviously not talking about having a live radio station. Instead, you can create and store your own radio station online. You can interview people from your industry and get them to give you their thoughts on different subjects.

This is a new thing, but I've already seen agents have success with it. They just tell prospective clients, "I'd like to give you the information on how to access my radio station. You can tune in whenever you want." Right away, the client's perception of the agent changes. It's a terrific option for an unfair advantage.

Speak Up

You can also build your breakthrough advantage just by speaking.

Speaking at association meetings can be very powerful. If there's a particular niche business that you're looking to get into, that business typically has its share of associations. You can find out what they are and go talk to them.

I did this myself when I first got into the business in Malibu. I used to go around to real estate offices in the area and ask when they were having their weekly or monthly meetings. Then I'd offer to drop in with some goodies—donuts, fruit, or whatever—and ask for two or three minutes to give everyone the state of the market as it related to insurance in the area.

And at the end of my talk, I always said, "I promise never to delay the close of escrow. If you call my office, I will make sure that you get your certificate of insurance by the time you need it, no matter what."

That hit home with a lot of Realtors. More than one of them had been in a position where escrow was about to close and they suddenly realized, "Oh my god, I never ordered the insurance." And that tiny two-minute speech was how I got people to call me. It only took a couple times for me to prove to them that I could come through, and then it was off to the races. Everyone knew that all they had to do was "Call Bart."

If you do get out there and speak, it's important to stay consistent about it. You don't want to pop into those kinds of meetings once or twice, because no one will remember you. But if you do them regularly, people start to recognize you. They start to know your name. Then you give them your tag line at the end of your speech, and that's when it sticks. That's when you get your unfair advantage.

Publish in the Paper

Local newspapers are another way to consider building your breakthrough advantage—especially if the niche market you're targeting is an older audience.

Reach out to your local paper and see if they'll let you do a column. Most local newspapers are always interested in getting information that is newsworthy and specific to that community. You can always find some sort of topic to write about that relates to insurance, whether it's about the Affordable Care Act, flood insurance during the rainy season, or fire insurance during fire season.

If you make your articles short and interesting, and if you tailor them to the community where you're doing business, you'll find that most editors are very receptive to the idea of letting you have a regular article in the paper. And the more the community becomes familiar with your name, the stronger your position as an expert becomes—and the bigger your unfair advantage gets.

Other Tools

The tools out there that you can use to create your breakthrough advantage are just about endless. There are podcasts, YouTube videos, video stories, whiteboard videos, telesummits, webinars, and live events or workshops, to name a few—and the list keeps growing every day.

Brainstorm until you find the tool that's right for you. Choose something that will be visible in the places where your ideal clients will actually be looking, and be as creative as possible. Just keep in mind that the end goal is to set yourself up as an expert in the industry, so that when you meet potential clients for the first time, you're already positioned to get their business.

People First

Throughout this book, I've emphasized the importance of building relationships with your customers. That relationship-driven interaction is a powerful breakthrough advantage in and of itself.

At my agency, we are hands-on with our clients, from the way we handle their annual Gap Elimination Process™ reviews to the way we answer the phones. Putting people first is a company value that we implement into every procedure and system in our office. It's not just something we do willy-nilly. It's a consistent method of operation, and that's why we're able to turn it into an unfair advantage.

For example, if a client experiences an emergency at two o'clock in the morning and calls the office, we have someone on call for that. The client hears the usual after-hours message, and in the message it says, "If this is an emergency claim, press 8." They press it and it goes to a twenty-four-hour answering service, and the service connects the client with whoever is on call that night.

Right away, the customer gets to talk to someone they know, who tells them, "I'm so sorry this happened to you. We are going to file this claim and get your car picked up," or calls the restoration service after a fire or whatever the disaster happens to be. The client remembers that we were there in their hour of need, and that connection goes a long way.

Our agency is full of services like that. Nothing is too small to take into consideration, because the little things compound upon one another to make the difference. We design our business specifically to foster relationships with our clients, and we see an enormous payoff from that in terms of retention and referrals. That's the real power of a breakthrough advantage.

Referrals: The Biggest Breakthrough Advantage of All

In this chapter, I've covered a number of ways to create an unfair advantage for your breakthrough insurance agency. But I've saved the biggest one for last: referrals.

Compared to someone who is trying to quote people by making cold calls, building a business where potential clients call *you* because they were referred by people whom they like and trust is the kind of unfair advantage that will not just give you an edge in the industry—it will transform your entire agency and catapult you to a level of success you've only dreamed of.

Referrals are so important that I've devoted an entire chapter to them, specifically—and it's coming up next.

⟨⟩⟨⟩⟨⟩

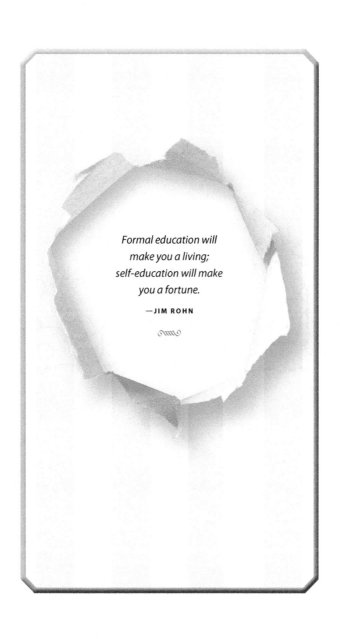

*Formal education will
make you a living;
self-education will make
you a fortune.*

—JIM ROHN

Chapter 9

Referrals: The Biggest Breakthrough of All

The Ollie's Duck & Dive Deal

The single biggest advantage of a breakthrough insurance agency is referrals.

One day, my wife and I were having lunch at a restaurant near the agency—Ollie's Duck & Dive—when I noticed that one of our clients was sitting right behind us.

So I turned around in my seat and said hello. "Hey, Steve," I greeted him. "How are you doing?"

"Bart," he smiled. "Good to see you. Let me introduce you to my good friend, David." The other man at Steve's table nodded his head, and I greeted him in return. Steve turned to David. "So, David, how big is your umbrella policy?" he asked.

David raised his eyebrows. "What are you talking about?" he said.

"You know, your umbrella policy," Steve explained. "Your liability umbrella. How big is it? I know you have a lot of cars and other exposures. If you don't have at least a $5 million umbrella policy, I think you're nuts."

"Well, Steve," David admitted, "I don't know that I have any umbrella policy at all."

Steve shook his head. "Are you kidding? Listen, David, you need to get one. I mean it. You have to promise me you'll take care of it today. As soon as we're done here, Bart is going to call you to make sure you get it in place. Here, Bart, take down David's number."

"Okay," I said. I was just sitting there, watching the whole conversation unfold in front of me. I got David's number and email address.

"Do you need anything else, Bart?" Steve asked.

"No, no. That should do it," I said.

"Good," Steve nodded. "Now listen, as soon as you're done setting it up, I want both of you to call me, understand? I want to make sure it gets done. It's that important."

"Sure, Steve. No problem," we agreed.

So after lunch, I went back to the office, and the first thing I did was personalize some rates for David's $5 million umbrella policy. Then I gave David a call. "Listen, I don't want to tick Steve off, so I've got this umbrella all set to put in place for you. Are we doing this by Visa or MasterCard?"

"Let's do Visa," David said.

Once that transaction was taken care of, I wished David a good day and called up Steve. "Okay Steve, David's umbrella policy is done. Thank you so much for the referral."

"Yeah, well, thank you for taking care of him," Steve replied. "I can't believe he didn't have an umbrella. Do you know he's one of the biggest doctors in Beverly Hills?" He started telling me all about David, and it turned out the two of them went way back. They'd been friends since childhood. Anything Steve said, David was going to take his advice.

David was in Steve's circle of influence. Steve was in mine. And that led to referred business for my agency.

Quote Shop versus Referral Shop

Referrals are one of my favorite things to talk about, because this is where you find the real difference between a transaction-based "quote shop" and a relationship-based "referral shop."

This is where the "breakthrough" of your breakthrough insurance agency really comes to life.

The difference between a quote shop and a referral shop is dramatic, to say the least. With a quote shop, 80 percent of your business is based on your marketing efforts, and only 20 percent of it is referred leads. You're cold calling and buying advertising. You put a lot of time and energy into these outbound efforts, and after all of that your closing ratio is maybe one or two out of ten people—*if* you're really good at it.

Compare that to a referral shop. With a referral shop, we flip those numbers: 80 percent of your business comes to you, and only 20 percent of it is outbound. You close eight out of ten of the people who come to you, and it only takes a fraction of the effort that the cold callers are putting in, because the people calling you up are already predisposed to like you. The efficiency and time savings are huge. And as an added bonus, you don't have to deal with the negativity of being rejected from all those cold calls.

And it gets even better. Most quote shops are so scattershot and spend so much money on their outbound efforts that they take home less than 30 percent of their gross income at the end of the day. With a referral shop—especially one that targets a good niche market—you can take home up to 45 percent or more of those same commissions while having a well-staffed office. That's a huge difference in income.

In other words, building a referral shop is a colossal unfair advantage over your competition—and a major key to creating your breakthrough insurance agency.

This chapter will show you how to grow your center of influence and manage your referral sources—two things that will enable your business to constantly propel itself to new heights.

Grow Your Center of Influence

Eventually, you want a significant part of your business to be about managing referrals. But you can't manage referrals until you start getting them in the first place. So how do you start up the referral trend?

You grow your center of influence.

This sounds hard, but it's actually much easier than most people think. Even if you're a brand-new agent with a lofty goal of eventually serving the higher end of the market, you can make this happen. You just have to be willing to work from the ground up.

It starts with having the right philosophy. If you believe that insurance is a commodity for which you're trying to get the least amount of coverage for the least amount of cost, you're not going to get very far. You need to look at insurance as a product that we are fortunate enough to be able to buy; one that allows us to transfer our risk exposure to an insurance company for a minimal amount of money.

You take this philosophy into your business with you, and you serve people with the honest intent of doing what's best for them. When you start out, maybe you'll be insuring teachers. Teachers matter, and it should matter to you that you're covering them correctly. Many of them don't have the right insurance. By providing that, you're giving them tremendous value. Along the way, you're demonstrating that you're likable, confident, and trustworthy.

Before long, those teachers will be in your immediate center of influence. And that's when they'll begin referring you out. You take those referrals and you do it all again; then you do it again, and again. Every now and then, you'll come across somebody whose assets are more substantial in nature, and you provide the same outstanding service to that person that you did to the teachers. Your circle of influence will start to include those higher earners.

Keep at it long enough, and eventually you'll flourish in the niche area that you want to be in. You just have to have the right mindset and be willing to put in the sweat equity, going into it.

The Referrer Rewards Program

When people do begin to send you referrals, you don't just sit there and say nothing about it. You need to recognize the person who went out of his or her way to give that referral to you—whether or not the referral itself actually resulted in a new customer. When you do this, it cements the relationship you have with that referrer, and it validates that they made the right decision by referring business to you.

So how do you go about cementing that relationship?

In my agency, I really like to give gifts. I send an email to the referrer right away, and I say, "Thank you so much for recommending John to the agency. We'll take really good care of him. I really appreciate the opportunity to be of service." But I don't leave it at that. I follow it up with a gift within a reasonable period of time, and that becomes the icing on the cake for them. It's the exclamation point that makes them think, "Wow, these people are a really classy act."

The gift you send is up to your judgment. You always want to send nice things, but you don't want to get lavish with it, because lavish could actually backfire on you—you don't want the recipient to feel that they're paying too much for their insurance.

At my agency, we spend between $30 and $100 on the average gift. Wine, flowers, concert tickets, massages, gift certificates to restaurants, and Starbucks cards are examples of some of the things we send to clients. Try to pay attention to what your clients like. If they don't drink wine, obviously the flowers are going to be a better idea. Always include a handwritten thank you card with the gift.

If you really want to go out of your way to recognize a client, a great way to do it is by "breaking bread." Take the person out to breakfast, lunch, or dinner. If they have a significant other, tell them to bring that individual along. Make it a very nice restaurant. Breaking bread creates a wonderful, informal atmosphere that builds trust and is a very powerful way to build a relationship. I really can't think of a better way to connect on a human level.

Remember, whatever you do, be genuine about it. Go into the gift strictly from a place of appreciation. If you operate in this manner, I guarantee that your referrals will increase, and you'll be able to divert money that you're using on old-fashioned traditional marketing to invest instead in recognizing your referral sources within the agency.

The A List

You need to recognize all of your referral sources. But over time, you'll find that some people will definitely refer more people to you than others, or that the quality of the referrals they send is pretty incredible. These are the people who need to go on your "A List."

In my agency, we keep a list of our A-List folks in our database, and we make sure to give them extra recognition. These people are very powerful centers of influence. They get special treatment: faster service and additional touch points throughout the year.

For example, we send thank you cards to anybody who refers us, regardless of who they are. But these top fifty people get something a little bit more special. On their birthdays, I'll call them personally, send them something special, or offer to take them out to lunch. If they're celebrating an anniversary or going on a trip, we acknowledge that with emails: "Happy anniversary," or "Have a good time in Normandy."

The point is that these people are intentionally recognized at a higher level, because they deserve to be. These are your platinum members; your frequent fliers. You need to make sure that they really feel appreciated in a big way. Their numbers should be in your cell phone contacts. You should send them postcards when you go on vacation. Everybody in your office should know who these people are.

Set up a system to make sure you recognize your A List on a regular basis. Again, the intention is honest gratitude. The byproduct is more business.

The Client On-Boarding Process

You'll find that the more you build strong relationships with your existing clients in general, the more referrals will start pouring in.

I have to say it again: This isn't something you do with the end result in mind. You build the relationships because you genuinely want to build them, for their own sake, without any thought of getting something out of it in return. And it just happens that when you go into it with this mindset, as the saying goes, "What goes around, comes around."

At my agency, we start and foster our customer relationships using what we call a client onboarding process. This is a system we have in place supported by a cloud-based program called lola-systems.com. Lola is a customer relationship management software that allows you to create online reminders for when you want to get in touch with your clients.

We programmed Lola to include ten touch points that we want every new client to get from us during the course of the first twelve months he or she is doing business with us. The first one is a thank you card. Then, after a certain amount of days, we follow that up with a telephone call, and so on and so forth throughout the year.

My staff takes care of most of the touch points. However, when the client hits the six-month mark, the touch point lands on my desk. It gives me the opportunity to personally thank that client for doing business with us, and that's important. The client feels an elevation of appreciation because the owner of the company knows and cares about him. It doesn't take a lot of my time, and it's a great way to solidify the relationship.

The important thing with relationship building is to stay consistent. The more you practice outreach on a regular basis with intention, the more likable, confident, and trustworthy you'll become to your clients. And that, my friends, is the holy grail when it comes to expanding your center of influence and attracting larger referral sources. Before long, people will be calling in and asking, "Where do I send the check?"

They know that you're the one they want to do business with before they ever exchange a word with you, just because so-and-so said so.

What Goes Around Comes Around

What goes around really does come around in this business. If you send around gratitude and genuine appreciation, that will come back to you in referrals. You can even funnel your own personal business to your clients. Given the choice, we'd all rather do business with someone who is doing business with us than with a total stranger.

So you want to give back to your clients whenever you can—and you also need to give back to the people who make your entire referral shop operation possible in the first place: your employees. In the next chapter, I'll give you a compensation structure for your staff that will allow them to share in the success of your breakthrough insurance agency so that it continues to flourish.

$\backsim\!\!\infty\!\!\sim$

Chapter 10

The Breakthrough
Compensation System

Don't Leave It on the Table

When you compensate your staff fairly, you don't just support them—you also support your business.

For years and years in my office, my staff was always after me to give them service commissions. "Why don't we get service commissions? All you give us is commissions on new business."

Now, they were already getting some good money from commissions on the new business alone. But I wanted them to be able to participate in the success of the business even more. And I had a personal goal in mind that I wanted to reach.

"Okay, look," I finally said, "here's my problem. I need more life insurance production. You're the ones who are talking to the majority of the customers on a regular basis. If you help me with the life insurance production, I'll give you service commission in turn. Here's how we're going to structure it…"

I told each department that if they sold one life insurance policy per month, they'd get 3 percent on service commissions. If they sold two per month, they'd get 6 percent, and if they sold three per month, they'd earn 10 percent. The departments agreed to the plan, and we got started.

Well, for the first two months after that, one of the departments skunked on life insurance.

At the end of the first month, we met for our usual production recap, and I laid a wide spread of hundred-dollar bills out on the table. "Well guys, this is what you didn't make in service commission this month. Honestly, I'm sorry to keep it with the agency. I'd really rather give it to you." Then I swept up the bills and put them away.

When it happened again the second month, I could feel the negativity rolling off of them. They weren't happy with themselves.

"You're really angry about this, aren't you?" I asked.

"As a matter of fact, we are," they grumbled.

"You know, I don't blame you," I commiserated. "I would be really angry, too. As hard as I work, to leave this amount of money on the table . . . I tell you, I wouldn't ever let it happen again. I'd make sure I have three life insurance policies next time around, because my family deserves the money." And I gathered the hundred-dollar bills and took them off the table a second time.

Well, that did it. They were incensed, and they were motivated. The next month, they sold one life insurance policy. The month after that, it was two. Then they hit three.

Now, that department brings in three life insurance policies almost every single month. I'm happy, because the agency is meeting its life insurance goals. And the service commission money hardly ever gets left on the table.

Value Your Staff

At this point in the process, your breakthrough insurance agency is really starting to take shape. You've learned how to leverage your vision and core qualities, how to grow your business with maximizers and multipliers, how to structure successful departments, and how to transform your agency from a quote shop into a referral shop.

Now, I'm going to teach you the piece of the program that pulls the whole thing together: how to compensate your staff so that they share in the success of the agency as it continues to thrive.

Time and time again, I hear about agents who try to grow their businesses by bringing on multipliers and throwing them into the deep end. They expect their multipliers to get their own leads, do their own marketing, and survive off of commissions, so of course the multipliers end up failing. They're new to the business. If they're supposed to figure all of that stuff out single-handedly, they might as well become agents themselves.

What you want is a compensation model where the team as a whole gets to participate in the success of the agency. You want to create transparency, so team members are 100 percent aware of where they stand, and you want to support them and give them the opportunity to earn bigger and bigger checks.

When you run things this way, people are happy. They're proud to be part of what you're doing, and they want to stay. In my decades of doing business, I have literally had only one person leave her position voluntarily, and that was because she was following a personal dream of hers, not because she felt undervalued. We don't lose people. I may let them go, or they may move away by necessity. But I've never had anybody quit on me because of compensation.

The compensation model outlined for you in this chapter will create a culture of success and prosperity in your organization. It will compensate your people generously without giving away the farm. If you have a slow month, your company won't take the brunt of the expense. If you have a great month, your staff will share in that success. It will give you the option of unlimited growth, without your fixed expenses ever becoming a burden.

This model will work for anyone, at any stage of the agency-building process. It is easy to communicate, administrate, and leverage as far as accomplishing the goals you have in place for your agency. Let me walk you through it a step at a time, from base salaries and commissions to additional benefits.

The Breakthrough Compensation Structure

Everyone in my agency participates in a commissions compensation structure: the more money the agency makes, the more money each person makes. The only thing I'm tied to is their base pay. The only exceptions are my receptionist in the claims concierge department and my contact manager, both of whom receive periodic raises instead.

Here is the full breakdown of my proven compensation structure, from base salaries to commissions.

Base Salaries

You begin with base salaries for your maximizers and multipliers. The base salary you set for each of those positions depends on the department and the area you operate in. For example, in my case, we have to draw from a hiring pool outside of the Malibu community.

They come from the surrounding areas, so I pay a little bit of a higher base salary to compensate them for the commute time—typically between $16 and $20 an hour.

You don't want to go nuts on base pay, because that is your fixed expense. If you're making more money, you don't mind paying more money; but if you're making less money, you don't want to pay more money. That's why, instead of giving raises on base pay, you offer a competitive commissions structure.

Commissions

As soon as a new hire passes the ninety-day probationary period, that individual becomes eligible to participate in commissions. You want to set up your commissions structure to take place on two levels: commissions on new business, and service commissions.

For any new business commissions that come in the door for a given department, set things up so that department gets 15 percent of the agency's income. For example, say that a personal lines sale resulted in $100 of commission for the agency. The personal lines department gets $15 of that $100, and the agency retains the other $85. Same thing for commercial sales.

It's important to note that it doesn't matter where the sale originated. Sometimes, I'm the one who talks to a client and closes a sale. Even if I handle it from beginning to end, the department it belongs to gets 15 percent of that transaction. As long as the new money is flowing through a department, that department gets the new business commission. I mentioned in chapter 5 that we set an $80,000 benchmark for our personal and commercial lines departments as a monthly goal. This is where that number comes from.

The other goal we set is three life insurance policies from each of those departments—and this is where the service commissions part of the equation comes into play.

Life insurance is something that carriers really benefit from, because it gives them stability of income for their bottom line. Whereas other products like home insurance go through huge fluctuations when storms or natural disasters strike, life insurance is a dependable constant for carriers, and they like us as their agents to support that model. It's also a product that hugely benefits consumers, as I can tell you from the millions and millions of dollars in benefit claims that I've personally handed out to clients over the years.

But life insurance isn't something that most people sign up for by default, since it's not required of them by lenders or state law. It takes more effort to sell it—and that's why you want to tie it to your team's service commissions as serious motivation to promote it.

Service commissions are commissions on policies that are being renewed, and obviously renewals make up the bulk of your agency's income. As I described at the beginning of this chapter, you want to align your service commissions rate with the number of life insurance policies that are sold. The model I use is 3 percent per department for one sold life insurance policy a month, 6 percent for two, and 10 percent for three. When a department sells three policies, that results in thousands of extra dollars for the people in those positions.

You also want to allow your departments to sell ahead, because this prevents sandbagging. I always tell my staff, "The best thing you can do is sell thirty-six policies in the month of January. Then you've got the whole year covered for service commissions." On a realistic level, if personal lines sells four life policies in February, that fourth policy carries over into March, and they have a head start that month.

So on any given day in my agency, the conversation is always about "80 and 3": $80,000 in new business, and three life insurance policies. The goals are clear, and they were a stretch at first, but I coached my staff. I pushed them and supported them, and now they're achieving those numbers on a regular basis.

Every time they do, they make more money. This is the kind of commissions structure that allows them to share in the business's success.

Splitting Commissions

Agents ask me all the time, "How do you split commissions? *Do* you split commissions?"

Yes, we do split commissions. I grew up in a restaurant business, and in the restaurant we had a tip-splitting model for the waiter and the busboy. When tips came in, the waiter got the bigger share—between 75 and 80 percent—and the busboy took the remaining 20 to 25 percent.

We use that exact same model in our agency. The multiplier gets 75 to 80 percent of the commissions that come in, and the maximizer takes the other 20 or 25 percent. If the maximizer is doing a phenomenal job, the multiplier gives that person a higher percentage. New maximizers typically start at 20 percent and then have the opportunity to reach the 25 percent commission mark. Eventually, those maximizers turn into multipliers and earn the bigger commission.

Everybody wins.

Additional Benefits

Beyond the base salary and commission structure, we offer our staff plenty of additional benefits.

We give them SEP IRAs. They can contribute up to $12,000 if they're under fifty, and up to $14,500 a year if they're over fifty. The agency matches their contributions with 3 percent of their salaries.

We also give everybody a $200 allowance to buy their own health insurance—which we find for them, because we're licensed and we have a department for that. Everyone on staff gets the usual paid holidays, sick days, and personal days.

We also take them to Las Vegas every year for a weekend. We invite them to bring their significant others, and we just play like rock stars: chauffeur-driven limousines, great shows, nice hotels, fancy restaurants—the works.

We have a great time, in and out of the office, and we all share in the prosperity that the agency brings.

Part of the Dream

I tell my staff members from the beginning, "It's my intention to never increase your base salary. I'll never give you a raise. But as the agency continues to do better, you're going to do better." And they do.

Compensation is important to my team, and that's the way it should be. I don't want people on my staff who aren't motivated by money, because that's a big driver of our success. But at the same time, money isn't the only thing that matters. In fact, it's not even the most important thing.

The people in my agency aren't just hired hands. They're part of the dream. They take a lot of pride in our company being one of the best in the industry. They love it when we win awards and make achievement clubs. They get a lot of satisfaction from knowing that they are helping to create and run a thriving, successful business.

They share the vision, and I always let them know how much I appreciate them and how special they are. They are the reason that we are where we are today.

Chapter 11

Your Breakthrough
Vision Now

Connect the Dots

The house I live in now overlooks the coast, with a pristine view of the Pacific Ocean. My neighbors include Grammy award-winning celebrities, Hollywood dealmakers, and entrepreneurial stars.

But sometimes, I like to drive by the old garage that we started in, the one that Wendy and I fixed up when we first arrived in Malibu, uncertain about how we would make it here. That old garage is only about a ten-minute drive from where I now live, yet it's a world away. Driving by, I am reminded that dreams do come true, that if you keep your mind on your goals, you will achieve them.

At that time, I didn't have a clear path to follow. When I entered the insurance business, I didn't have a plan or system for growth. Now, I do. As Steve Jobs once said, "You can't connect the dots looking forward; you can only connect them looking backwards. So you have to trust that the dots will somehow connect in your future."

For me, those dots looking backwards became the Breakthrough Insurance Agency system I have shared with you in this book.

The Road from Here

Now you can connect the dots. You can create a stronger future using this system. You are equipped with the understanding that you need to build success for yourself in this industry. There's only one thing left to do: get out on the road and start walking.

But you have a lot to do, and trying to implement every single process I've discussed at the same time may sound overwhelming. It could even turn out to be ineffective to bite off more than your ready to chew, all at once. The best way to approach it is to pick one or two systems and start putting them in place, with the goal of integrating all of them into your breakthrough agency, eventually.

So where do you go from here? What are your immediate next steps to turning this game plan into your real-life success story?

The answer depends on where you are in your journey as an agent: closer to the beginning, middle, or end of the road.

Where to Start: New Agent

If you're a new agent, you're actually at an advantage as far as systems go, because you get to start with a clean slate. You don't have any bad habits to break or any "broken machinery" to scrap before you can rebuild.

You can use my breakthrough process to build your agency from the very beginning.

Work with the chapters of this book in order. Start with your vision. Remember that you cannot become larger than the vision you see for yourself, and that you will constantly expand that vision as you go along. Develop your personal qualities of likability, confidence, and trustworthiness.

Then, when you're ready, start growing your team using the processes I've outlined here. Refer back to the chapters again as you're putting each system into place. If you are seriously looking to jumpstart your business and put your agency on the fast track to breakthrough status, deepen your education by attending my workshops.

There are two pieces of advice I received when I was starting out in business that helped me above all others. The first was from a mentor of mine, Wilfred Schwartz, and the second was from my father. When I asked Wilfred Schwartz his secret for success, he told me, "Look for opportunity, and when you find it, take advantage of it." The second piece of advice, from my father, was "Start and continue."

Don't be afraid to start where you are. Put the sweat equity into your business when you're starting out. Look for opportunity. When you find it, take advantage of it. Then start and continue.

Where to Start: Experienced Agent

Now let's say you're an agent with some experience, but you haven't made it big yet. You're in the thick of things, and you're looking for a way to break through. Where do you begin?

If you're already working in the industry, chances are that you're operating with a traditional structure in place. You might have a compensation model that's all over the board. Maybe your multipliers get 100 percent of the new business commission coming in, and you as the agent are just hoping to get a renewal commission on the back end. Maybe you're only netting 20 or 25 percent at the end of the day, or maybe things are so tangled up that you aren't even sure what you're netting at all.

If any of this sounds familiar, the first thing to implement is a new compensation structure. Shift your paradigm so that your employees are participating in the growth of the agency through department commissions.

Help your team transition into this. You don't want to scare them and tell them that you're reducing their incomes when they have financial commitments they have to make. Sit down with them and show them the new structure. Let them see how their income would have performed on this new system, historically, and how it stands to perform in the future as far as potential. Be completely transparent about it: the more money the agency makes, the more money they get. They may end up making more money than they were before.

Some people may not get behind you in what you're looking to accomplish, and if that's the case you may need to make the hard choice to move forward without them. That's okay. There's nothing wrong with that. You are the owner of your business, and you're not going to be held hostage by somebody who has a different agenda than you.

From there, revamp your operations. Instead of each of your team members being an island, give them complete support. Funnel business to them. If they're not already producing life insurance for you, motivate them to do that by tying it to their service commissions structure. Set stretch-number goals that are still achievable, and get everyone working as a team to reach them.

Once those fundamentals are in place, set up your review process and begin managing your referral sources. This will put you on the fast track to becoming a "referral shop" agency, where the phone rings off the hook all day long with people wanting to do business with you.

When you take these steps, you'll change from being the responsible party in your business to being the support position. And that will free up your time to allow you to devote your attention to new areas of growth.

Where to Start: Advanced Agent

At the other end of the spectrum, if you're already an established agent who is doing well, you may have plateaued and are looking for ways to take your agency to the next level.

If that's the case, you'll want to head straight for the fine-tuning techniques to generate some more specific results. Odds are you know what those results are, and you already have a sense of which techniques resonate with you as far as creating your unfair breakthrough advantage. Pick them up, try them out, and have a lot of fun blowing your old records out of the water.

Build Your Network

Whatever level you happen to be at, you'll find that you'll get a lot of benefit from the information you've just learned, going forward. But it doesn't stop here. You can get an equally large amount of benefit from building your network.

I was big on this when I started out. I always wanted to talk to other people who were successful or working toward success in the business, and that was an incredible education for me. Get out there and network with other individuals who are in your position or already operating at a higher level. Find and meet those people. Hang out with them, talk to them, and learn from their challenges and successes. You'll come away with a thousand new ideas that had never crossed your mind before.

You can get instant access to this community of industry peers and join my personal network by participating in my workshops. I've done my best to cover my process in this book, but there's only so much information that will fit in a 135-page book. The workshops are designed to give you specific in-depth resources and step-by-step guidelines that will help you take the processes in this overview to new heights.

Remember, you are the mean average of the five people you surround yourself with. Choose to surround yourself with good ones.

Enjoy the Ride

There is no greater joy in life than to feel free and happy. In reality, money—or an adequate income—plays a huge role in our feeling of freedom. When we have time to enjoy it, there is an elevation of happiness.

As the saying goes, money in itself doesn't do anything. It just makes you more of what you already are.

I know in my heart from over twenty-five years in this business that what you've learned in these pages will help you to increase your income and reduce the amount of time that you personally have to spend to do so. If, like me, your byproduct is an increased level of happiness, I will have more than accomplished what I set out to do.

I am grateful and appreciative for the time you have spent to learn the systems that have worked so well for our agency. Now, it's your turn to take them out for a spin. Go big and have fun!

⟨٥٧٥٥⟩

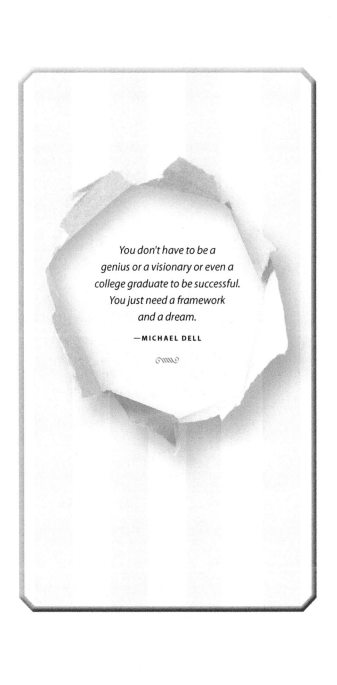

*You don't have to be a
genius or a visionary or even a
college graduate to be successful.
You just need a framework
and a dream.*

—MICHAEL DELL

About the Author

Bart Baker leads one of the most successful insurance agencies in the country. He and his wife, Wendy, run B.W. Baker Insurance, which has earned the Farmers Insurance Presidents Council accolade for the top 1 percent of producers in the nation every year since 2002. His agency has also earned Court of the Table and Top of the Table from the million-dollar roundtable multiple times.

Baker is a highly sought-after speaker and trainer with more than twenty-five years in the business. His business is consistently in the top 1 percent of Farmers agencies in the nation as far as income, bringing in $20 million a year in gross written premium in 2014. In addition to the Presidents Council award, B.W. Baker Insurance has also earned the Championship and Toppers recognitions from Farmers consistently since 1998.

Baker and his wife built their business and raised their three children in Malibu, California, where they still reside.

In reading this book, I hope that you have gained knowledge that will better prepare you for a successful future in the insurance business. I appreciate the time you've invested in furthering your insurance education.

I would also welcome the chance to share more detailed information and specific exercises to help you build your breakthrough insurance agency in my workshops. Please go to bwbakertraining.com for specifics on upcoming workshops.

For more information please contact us at:

B.W. Baker Insurance
www.bwbaker.com
29169 Heathercliff Road, Suite 208
Malibu, CA 90265
bart@bwbaker.com
(310) 457-5092